MW01120786

American
ENGLISH FILE

Christina Latham-Koenig
Clive Oxenden
Paul Seligson

Paul Seligson and Clive Oxenden are the original co-authors of
English File 1 and *English File 2*

OXFORD
UNIVERSITY PRESS

Contents

G simple past of *be*: was / were
V word formation: *paint > painter*
P sentence stress

Who was she? She was a famous actress.

7A At the National Portrait Gallery

1 GRAMMAR *was / were*

a Read about the National Portrait Gallery in Washington, D.C. and answer the questions.

1 Where is it?
2 What can you see there?
3 When is it open?
4 How much does it cost?

b (3 43)) Look at a photo that is in the National Portrait Gallery. Cover the dialogue and listen. Who are the two people in the photo?

> **A** I love that photo. Who are they?
> **B** I think it's President Ronald Reagan and his wife Nancy. Let's see. Yes, that's right.
> **A** When was he president?
> **B** He was president from 1981 to 1989. He was an actor, too.
> **A** Really? What movies was he in?
> **B** He was in *Dark Victory* with Bette Davis, a very famous actress in the 1930s and 1940s. He was also in movies with stars like Errol Flynn, Clark Gable, and Ginger Rogers.
> **A** Was Nancy an actress, too?
> **B** Yes, she was. They were in a movie together in 1957.
> **A** Were Ronald and Nancy happy?
> **B** I think they were very happy. They were together all their lives.

c Listen again and read the dialogue. Then fill in the blanks.

Simple present	Simple past
He is the president.	He _____ the president.
She is an actress.	She _____ an actress.
They are happy.	They _____ happy.

d ➤ p.136 Grammar Bank 7A. Learn more about *was / were* and practice it.

The National Portrait Gallery

The National Portrait Gallery has a collection of portraits of famous American men and women from the 17th century to the present day. The portraits are both paintings and photographs. The National Portrait Gallery is in Washington, D.C., a short walk from the National Mall. It is open daily and admission is free.

2 PRONUNCIATION & SPEAKING
sentence stress

a (3 45)) Listen and repeat. Copy the rhythm.

+ I was at a **party**.   She was **born** in **Mexico**.
My **parents** were **angry**.

− He **wasn't** at **home**.   They **weren't** very **happy**.

? **When** were you **born**?   **Where** was the **hotel**?
Was it **expensive**? **No**, it **wasn't**.
Were they at the **concert**? **Yes**, they **were**.

b (3 46)) Say the sentences in the simple past.

)) I'm at home. (I was at home.

c ➤ **Communication** *Where were you?* **A** *p.103* **B** *p.108*.

3 READING

a Look at three more pictures from the National Portrait Gallery. Do you know who the people are or anything about them?

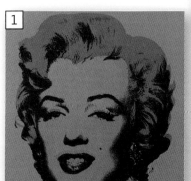

b (**3 47**)) Read and listen to three audio guide extracts. Check your answers to **a**.

1   Marilyn Monroe was born in Los Angeles, California in 1926. When she was a child, her life was very hard. Her mother was sick, and her father wasn't there very much. Marilyn was a factory worker and a model before she was an actress. Marilyn's three husbands were very important to her during her life. Her first husband was a sailor, the second was a famous baseball player, Joe DiMaggio, and the last was a famous writer, Arthur Miller.

2   Mary Wilson, Diana Ross, and Florence Ballard were born in the 1940s in Detroit, Michigan. Together they were The Supremes, a pop and soul singing group during the 1960s. All three women were very talented singers. In 1965, the Supremes were the first all-female singing group to have a number one album in the US. Their music was popular with everyone—men and women, teens and adults—and it is still popular today.

3   Thomas Edison, an inventor and businessman, was born in Ohio in 1847. At 13, he was an excellent salesperson selling candy and newspapers to train passengers. Later, he was the inventor of the incandescent light bulb, a movie camera, and the phonograph. Edison was also the owner of many companies, and some of them are in business today, e.g., General Electric. He was the loving husband of two wives—Mary Stillwell (1855–1884) and Mina Miller (1865–1947)—and the father of six children.

c Read the texts again and answer the questions.

1 Why was Marilyn's life hard when she was a child?
2 Who were Joe DiMaggio and Arthur Miller?
3 Were there any men in The Supremes?
4 Why is The Supreme's music still popular today?
5 What was Thomas Edison good at when he was a boy?
6 Who was Thomas's second wife?

d Cover the texts. What can you remember?

4 VOCABULARY word formation

a Find words in the texts for people made from these words:

1 act _____ (OR actor)   5 sing _____
2 sail _____   6 business _____
3 play _____   7 design _____
4 write _____   8 invent _____

> 🔍 **Word building: professions**
> We often add -er or -or to a verb, e.g., writer, actor.
> We often add -ian, -ist, or -man/woman to a noun, e.g., musician.

b Are the words below verbs or nouns? Do you know the words for the people?

1 dance _____   6 novel _____
2 compose _____   7 sports _____
3 politics _____   _____
4 science _____   8 paint _____
5 direct movie _____   9 art _____
       10 music _____

c (**3 48**)) Listen and check. Underline the stressed syllable. Practice saying the words.

d Write the names of four famous people in each circle. Ask a partner.

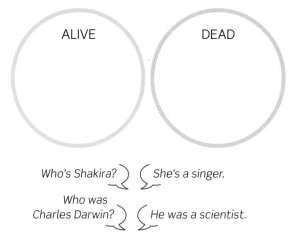

ALIVE   DEAD

Who's Shakira?   *She's a singer.*
Who was Charles Darwin?   *He was a scientist.*

5 LISTENING & WRITING

a (**3 49**)) Listen to five clues about two famous people. Do you know who they are?

b With a partner, write clues about a famous man and a woman (both dead).

c Read your clues to another pair. Do they know the people?

G simple past: regular verbs
V past time expressions
P *-ed* endings

7B Chelsea girls

What did they want to do?

They wanted to go to the match.

1 READING & LISTENING

a (3 50)) Read and listen to the true story about a trip. Number the sentences 1–7.

- [ ] The taxi arrived at the girls' house.
- [ ] They looked out of the window.
- [ ] They chatted and listened to music.
- [1] The girls wanted to go to a match.
- [ ] The taxi stopped in a street with pretty houses.
- [ ] They called a taxi.
- [ ] The taxi driver typed their destination into his GPS.

b (3 51)) Listen and check. Do you think they were in London?

c (3 52)) Listen to the news story on the radio. Where were they?

d ▶ **Communication** *Stamford Bridge p.103.* Read some tourist information about the place they were in and look at the map.

e Do you think it is easy to make a mistake like this? Whose fault was it?

2 GRAMMAR

simple past: regular verbs

a Read the text again and highlight ten more simple past regular verbs ⊞, one simple past negative sentence ⊟, and one simple past question ⍰.

b In pairs, complete the chart and answer questions 1–3.

Simple present	Simple past
They want to go to the match.	They _____ to go to the match.
They don't talk to the taxi driver.	They _____ to the taxi driver.
Where do you want to go?	Where _____ to go?

1 What letters do you add to a regular verb in the simple past, e.g., *call*?

2 What do you do if the verb ends in *e*, e.g., *type*?

3 What happens to verbs that end with one vowel and one consonant, e.g., *chat, stop*?

c ▶ **p.136 Grammar Bank 7B.** Learn more about simple past regular verbs and practice them.

Althorp House

The *taxi* trip

The Spencer sisters

Charles Spencer, Princess Diana's brother, has three daughters, 18-year-old Kitty, and 15-year-old twins Eliza and Amelia. They live in Althorp, a large country house near Northampton, about 85 miles (136 kilometers) north of London.

One of the sisters and her friend wanted to go to a soccer match in London. It was a Premier League match between Chelsea and Arsenal at Stamford Bridge. They called a taxi to take them to London and back. The taxi arrived and the driver typed Stamford Bridge into his GPS. The girls relaxed in the back of the car. They probably chatted, listened to music on their iPods, and texted their friends. They didn't talk to the taxi driver.

Two hours later the taxi stopped. They looked out of the window. It was a street with pretty houses.

The girls were a little surprised, and they asked the taxi driver where they were. "In Stamford Bridge," he said. "Where did you want to go?"

Stamford Bridge Stadium

d Stand up and move around the class. Ask *Did you… yesterday?* questions with the verb phrases below. When somebody answers *Yes, I did*, write his or her name.

YESTERDAY

Find a person who...

- used a GPS _____
- watched a soccer match _____
- chatted online _____
- studied for an exam _____
- texted a friend _____
- arrived at work / school late _____
- listened to the radio _____
- started a new book _____
- worked / studied until late _____
- played a computer game _____

Did you use a GPS yesterday?) (*No, I didn't. Did you...?*

3 PRONUNCIATION *-ed* endings

> **Simple past regular verbs**
> The *e* in *-ed* is not usually pronounced, and *-ed* is pronounced /d/ or /t/, e.g., *closed* /kloʊzd/, *stopped* /stɑpt/. The *-ed* is pronounced /ɪd/ **only** in verbs that end with the sound /t/ or /d/, e.g., *waited* /ˈweɪtɪd/, *ended* /ˈɛndɪd/.

a ③ 54)) Listen and repeat the verbs.

1 *-ed* = /d/	2 *-ed* = /t/	3 *-ed* = /ɪd/
called	looked	wanted
arrived	relaxed	chatted
listened	stopped	texted

b ③ 55)) Look at the verbs in the list. Circle the ones that belong to group 3. Listen and check.

played finished started traveled asked missed
cooked needed watched lived liked typed

c ③ 56)) Listen to some verb phrases. Make true ⊞ or ⊟ sentences about yesterday.

)) *play tennis* (*I played tennis yesterday. / I didn't play tennis yesterday.*

4 VOCABULARY & SPEAKING
past time expressions

a Number the past time expressions 1–10.

- ☐ yesterday morning
- ☐ last night
- ☐ last month
- ☐ three days ago
- ☐ *1* five minutes ago
- ☐ last week
- ☐ last summer
- ☐ the day before yesterday
- ☐ a year ago
- ☐ in 2009

> **Past time expressions**
> We say *last week, last month* NOT ~~the last week, the last month.~~

b ③ 57)) Listen and check. Then listen and repeat.

c Look at the questionnaire below. Tell your partner true sentences with past time expressions. Ask for more information.

I cried at the end of a movie last week.) (*Oh, really? What was it?*

When was the last time you...?

- ✱ cried at the end of a movie
- ✱ traveled by plane
- ✱ started a new hobby
- ✱ walked more than 5 miles
- ✱ booked a flight online
- ✱ downloaded a song
- ✱ played a sport
- ✱ missed an English class

- ✱ watched a really good movie
- ✱ called a friend
- ✱ danced

G simple past: irregular verbs
V *go, have, get*
P sentence stress

What did you do?

We went to a restaurant.

7C A night to remember

1 READING

a Look at the photos and read the introduction to the article. For each photo, say why you think the night was memorable.

b Read about two people's nights, and match them to a photo.

c Read the texts again and match the questions to their answers in the texts.

☐ What time did you get back?	☐ What did you wear?
☐ What was the weather like?	☐ Who were you with?
☐ Why was it a memorable night?	☐ What did you do?
☐ When was it? Where were you?	

Why do we remember some nights in our lives?

Is it because we went to a beautiful place, met interesting people, heard wonderful music, or saw a fantastic movie? We asked people all over the world to tell us about a night that they can never forget...

Maggie from the US

1 It was in February when I went to New York City.

2 I was with my family, and it was my sister's birthday. She wanted to see a Broadway show, and my favorite actor, Nick Jonas, was the star. So my dad got tickets and organized a surprise meeting with Nick after the show.

3 I felt pretty. I wore a black dress and a red coat and warm, black boots.

4 It was a cold and cloudy night.

5 After the show, many people were at the side door. Then a theater worker opened the door and Nick Jonas came out! We were really excited because he spoke to us and said happy birthday to my sister! We took some pictures with Nick, and then he left.

6 We went back to our hotel at 11 p.m.

7 It was an amazing evening! I saw a great show and met my favorite actor. And my sister had a memorable birthday.

Mehmet from Turkey

1 It was last year. I was in Istanbul, where I live.

2 I was with my friends. It was my best friend's birthday.

3 I wore a black T-shirt and blue jeans.

4 It was a hot night, and the water was really warm.

5 We went to a great place called Cezayir. It's an old building with a great restaurant. We had dinner, and after dinner we had a coffee. Then we went to the beach at Florya and swam in the ocean. It was fantastic. The water wasn't very clean, but we didn't mind!

6 After our swim, we were tired and decided to go back, but I couldn't find my car keys! We went back to the beach and we looked everywhere, but it was too dark. In the end, I left the car at the beach and I went home in my friend's car! I got home really late, at 5:00 in the morning.

7 It was a memorable night because we had a fantastic dinner and took a great swim, but also because I lost the car keys – it was my father's car and he was really angry!

2 GRAMMAR simple past: irregular verbs

a Look at the article again and find the past tense of these irregular verbs.

can	<u>could</u>	/kʊd/
come	_____	/keɪm/
feel	_____	/fɛlt/
get	_____	/ɡɑt/
go	_____	/wɛnt/
have	_____	/hæd/
hear	_____	/hərd/
leave	_____	/lɛft/
lose	_____	/lɔst/
meet	_____	/mɛt/
see	_____	/sɔ/
speak	_____	/spoʊk/
swim	_____	/swæm/
take	_____	/tʊk/
wear	_____	/wɔr/

b ③58))) Listen and check. Practice saying the verbs.

c ➤ **p.136 Grammar Bank 7C.** Learn more about simple past irregular verbs and practice them.

d Work in pairs. **A** re-read the text about Maggie. **B** re-read the text about Mehmet.

e ➤ **Communication** *A night to remember* **A** *p.103* **B** *p.108.* Test your partner's memory. Whose night do you think was more fun?

3 LISTENING

a You are going to listen to David from Spain talking about his memorable night. Look at photo **C** from **1**. Where was he? Why was it a memorable night?

b ③60))) Listen and check.

c Listen again. Correct the information.

1 It was on August 11th. *No, it was on July 11th.*
2 He was in Buenos Aires.
3 He watched the match in a hotel room.
4 He wore a Spanish soccer shirt and a yellow scarf.
5 The match was in the evening.
6 There were a lot of American tourists there.
7 After the match, they went to a restaurant downtown.
8 It was very cold that night.
9 He got to the hotel at 4:00 in the morning.

4 VOCABULARY go, have, get

a Can you remember these phrases about Mehmet? Write *went*, *had*, or *got*.

1 We ___ to a great place called Cezayir.
2 We ___ dinner, and after dinner we ___ a coffee.
3 Then we ___ to the beach at Florya.
4 I ___ home really late, at 5:00 in the morning.

b ➤ **p.160 Vocabulary Bank** *go, have, get.*

5 PRONUNCIATION sentence stress

a Look at the questions in "A memorable night" below. What words are missing?

b ③62))) Listen and repeat the questions. Copy the rhythm.

A memorable night...

- When / it?
- Where / you?
- Who / with?
- What / wear?
- Where / go?
- What / do?
- What / the weather like?
- What time / get home?
- Why / it a memorable night?

6 SPEAKING & WRITING

a Think about a time you had a memorable night. Look at the questions in **5b** and plan your answers.

b Interview your partner about his or her night.

c Write about your night. Answer the questions in **5b**, and use the article in **1** to help you.

7 ③63))) SONG *Summer Nights* ♫

1 🎥 VIDEO A FREE MORNING

a **(3 64)))** Rob and Jenny are planning what to do on their free morning. Watch or listen once. What is the problem?

b Watch or listen again. Complete the sentences with a word, a name, or a number.

1 Rob suggests that they go _____.
2 He says that they can _____ bikes.
3 _____ calls _____.
4 Rob needs to interview an _____.
5 Rob asks if he can do the interview on _____.
6 Rob and Jenny arrange to meet at _____ o'clock outside the Tate Modern*.

> 🔍 **Cultural note**
> * The Tate Modern is a famous art gallery in London.

2 VOCABULARY directions

a Match the words and pictures.

☐ on the <u>corner</u> /ˈkɔrnər/
☐ at the <u>traffic lights</u> /ˈtræfɪk laɪts/
☐ a bridge /brɪdʒ/
☐ across (from) /əˈkrɔs/
☐ turn left /tərn lɛft/
☐ turn right /tərn raɪt/
☐ go straight ahead /streɪt əˈhɛd/
☐ go past (the church) /pæst/

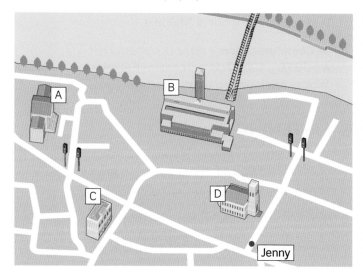

b **(3 65)))** Listen and check.

3 🎥 VIDEO ASKING THE WAY

a **(3 66)))** Jenny is trying to find the Tate Modern. Watch or listen. Is it A, B, C, or D?

b Watch or listen again. Complete the **You Hear** phrases.

You Say 💬	🔊 You Hear
Excuse me, please. Where's the Tate Modern?	_____, I don't live here.
Excuse me. Is the Tate Modern near here?	The Tate Modern? It's near here, but I don't know exactly _____. Sorry.
Thank you.	
Excuse me. Can you tell me the way to the Tate Modern, please?	Yes, of course. Go straight on. Go _____ the church. Then turn _____ at the traffic lights. And it's at the end of the street.
Sorry, could you say that again, please?	Yes, go straight on. Go _____ the church. Then turn _____ at the traffic lights. And it's at the end of the street. You can't _____ it!
Thank you.	

c (3 67)🔊 Watch or listen and repeat the **You Say** phrases. Copy the <u>rhy</u>thm.

d Practice the dialogue with a partner.

> 🔍 **Can you...? or Could you...?**
> *Can you tell me the way to the Tate Modern?*
> *Could you say that again, please?*
>
> We can use *Can you...?* Or *Could you...?* when we want to ask another person to do something.
> *Could you...?* is more polite.

e 👥 In pairs, role-play the dialogue. **A** ask for directions to building A (the library). Start with *Excuse me, where's...?* **B** give directions. Then change roles. Ask for directions to building C (the post office).

4 🎥 VIDEO **JENNY AND ROB GO SIGHTSEEING**

a (3 68)🔊 Watch or listen to Jenny and Rob. Mark the sentences **T** (true) or **F** (false).

1 The Millennium Bridge is for cars and people.
2 It was the first new bridge over the Thames in 100 years.
3 Rob interviewed the engineer last year.
4 Jenny doesn't like Shakespeare.
5 Daniel calls and invites Jenny to dinner.
6 Jenny accepts the invitation.
7 There's a gift shop on the top floor of the Tate Modern.
8 The Tate Modern was a power station until 1981.

b Watch or listen again. Say why the **F** sentences are false.

c Look at the **Social English phrases**. Who says them: **J**enny, **R**ob, or **D**aniel?

> **Social English phrases**
>
> | | |
> |---|---|
> | What a view! | What would you like to visit? |
> | What is there to see? | We could go to the Globe Theatre. |
> | Would you like to meet for lunch? | That's really nice of you. |
> | Maybe another time? | Yes, of course. |
>
> **American and British English**
>
> | | |
> |---|---|
> | *go straight ahead* = American English | *go straight on* = British English |
> | *across from* =American English | *opposite* = British English |

d (3 69)🔊 Watch or listen and check. Do you know what they are in your language?

e Watch or listen again and repeat the phrases.

> 👤 **Can you...?**
> ☐ ask for and understand directions
> ☐ give simple directions
> ☐ ask someone to do something in a polite way

G simple past: regular and irregular
V irregular verbs
P simple past verbs

8A A murder story

Did you hear anything during the night?

No, I didn't. I was very tired.

1 READING

a Read the back cover of a murder story. Then cover it and look at the photographs. Can you remember who the people are?

Who's Amanda? She's Jeremy's wife.

b (4 2)) Read and listen to the story. Mark the sentences **T** (true) or **F** (false). Correct the **F** sentences.

1 Somebody killed Jeremy between 12:00 a.m. and 2:00.
2 The detective questioned Amanda in the living room.
3 Jeremy went to bed before Amanda.
4 Amanda and Jeremy slept in the same room.
5 Somebody opened and closed Amanda's door.
6 Amanda got up at 7:00.
7 Amanda didn't love Jeremy.

c Look at the highlighted irregular verbs in the story. What are the base forms?

1 was = be

2 PRONUNCIATION
simple past verbs

a (4 3)) Listen to the pronunciation of these verbs in the simple past.

sat	could	found	heard	read
said	saw	took	wore	

b (4 4)) Now match the verbs in **a** with a word below that rhymes. Listen and check. Practice saying the words.

book _____   four _____
round _____   draw _____
bird _____   cat _____
good _____   bed _____ _____

c (4 5)) Find and underline nine simple past **regular** verbs in the story. How do you pronounce them? Listen and check.

Murder in a country house

June 22, 1958 was Jeremy Travers's sixtieth birthday. He had dinner at his country house with his wife Amanda, his daughter Barbara, his business partner Gordon, and his assistant Claudia. The next morning when Amanda Travers went to her husband's bedroom, she found him in bed...dead.

ISBN 978-0-19-459858-9

Claudia   *Gordon*

Detective Granger arrived at about 9:00. He [1]was a tall man with a big black mustache. Amanda, Barbara, Claudia, and Gordon [2]were in the living room. The detective [3]came in.

"Mr. Travers died between midnight last night and seven o'clock this morning," he [4]said. "Somebody in this room killed him." He looked at them one by one, but nobody [5]spoke.

"Mrs. Travers, I want to talk to you first. Come into the library with me, please."

Amanda Travers followed the detective into the library and they [6]sat down.

"What did your husband do after dinner last night?"

"When we finished dinner, Jeremy said he was tired and he [7]went to bed."

"Did you go to bed then?"

"No, I didn't. I went for a walk in the yard."

"What time did you go to bed?"

"About quarter to twelve."

"Was your husband asleep?"

Jeremy

Amanda

Barbara

"I don't know, Detective. We…we ⁸slept in separate rooms. But I ⁹saw that his door was closed."

"Did you hear anything when you were in your room?"

"Yes, I ¹⁰heard Jeremy's bedroom door. It opened. I ¹¹thought it was Jeremy. Then it closed again. I ¹²read in bed for half an hour and then I went to sleep."

"What time did you get up this morning?"

"I ¹³got up at about 7:15. I ¹⁴had breakfast and at 8:00 I ¹⁵took my husband a cup of tea. I ¹⁶found him in bed. He was…dead."

"Tell me, Mrs. Travers, did you love your husband?"

"Jeremy is…was a difficult man."

"But did you love him, Mrs. Travers?"

"No, Detective. I hated him."

3 LISTENING

a **4 6, 7, 8**))) Listen to the detective question Barbara. Write the information in the chart. Listen again and check. Then do the same for Gordon and Claudia.

	Amanda	*Barbara*	*Gordon*	*Claudia*
What did they do after dinner?	*She went for a walk.*			
What time did they go to bed?	*11:45.*			
Did they hear anything?	*Jeremy's door opened and closed.*			
Possible motive?	*She hated him.*			

b Compare your chart with a partner. Who do you think was the murderer: Amanda, Barbara, Gordon, or Claudia? Why?

c **4 9**))) Now listen to what happened. Who was the murderer? Why did he / she kill Mr. Travers? Were you right?

4 GRAMMAR simple past: regular and irregular

a Cover the story and look at these verbs. Are they regular or irregular in the simple past? Write the simple past form ⊞ and ⊟ for each verb.

~~come~~ kill close speak sleep sit hate walk

⊞ *came* ⊟ *didn't come*

b **4 10**))) Listen and check.

c ▶ **p.138 Grammar Bank 8A.** Learn more about simple past regular and irregular verbs and practice them.

d ▶ **p.165 Irregular verbs** Check (✓) the irregular verbs you know. Choose three new ones and learn them.

5 SPEAKING

▶ **Communication** *Police interview* **A** *p.104* **B** *p.108.* Interview robbery suspects. Are they telling the truth?

G *there is / there are, some / any* + plural nouns
V the house
P /ɛr/ and /ɪr/, sentence stress

Is there a garage?

Yes, there is.

8B A house with a history

1 VOCABULARY the house

a Read the advertisement about a house for rent. Would you like to rent it? Why (not)?

b Cover the advertisement. What can you remember about the house?

c With a partner, think of three things you can usually find in a bedroom, a bathroom, and a living room.

d ➤ **p.161 Vocabulary Bank** *The house.*

FOR RENT

Beautiful country house.
Very quiet. Six bedrooms, four bathrooms, large yard. Five miles from town. Perfect family house.

LOW PRICE.

2 LISTENING

a (**4 13**)) Kim and Leo are a young couple. They want to rent the house in **1**. Cover the dialogue and listen to their conversation with Barbara. Which three rooms in the house do they go into?

b Listen again and complete the dialogue.

> **K** The yard is wonderful. I love it.
> **L** Is there a ¹*garage*?
> **B** Oh yes, there's a big garage over there. Let's go inside the house.
>
>   This is the ²_____. There are five rooms on this floor: the kitchen, the ³_____, the living room, the ⁴_____, the library...
> **L** Wow! There's a library, Kim!
> **B** This is the living room.
> **L** I love the furniture—the old sofa, the armchairs, the ⁵_____...
> **B** And this is the ⁶_____. It's very big, as you can see.
> **K** Is there a dishwasher?
> **B** No, there isn't. It's an old house, you see.
> **L** Never mind. I think it's nice. Is there a ⁷_____ downstairs?
> **B** Yes, there's one ⁸_____ and there are three upstairs.
> **K** Are there any ⁹_____ with children?
> **B** No, there aren't any neighbors near here. But there are some families with children in town.
> **K** That's great. You lived in this house, is that right, Mrs...?
> **B** Call me Barbara, dear. Yes, I lived here. A long time ago. Now I live in town. Let's go ¹⁰_____...

c (**4 14**)) Listen. What does Kim say about one of the bedrooms? Whose bedroom was it?

d (4 15)) Kim and Leo go to a local restaurant. Listen and answer the questions.

1 What do they have to drink? Why?
2 What does the waiter tell them…?
  a about what happened in the house
  b about Barbara
  c about what happened to the house later
3 What do Kim and Leo decide to do?

3 GRAMMAR *there is / there are*

a In groups of three, practice the dialogue in **2b**. Then complete the chart.

	singular	plural
+	There's a yard.	There ____ some families in town.
−	There ____ a dishwasher.	There aren't any neighbors.
?	____ ____ a garage?	____ ____ any neighbors?

b What's the difference between…?

1 There are **three** families in town.
2 There are **some** families in town.

c ➤ **p.138 Grammar Bank 8B.** Learn more about *there is / there are*, etc., and practice it.

4 PRONUNCIATION
/ɛr/ and /ɪr/, sentence stress

a (4 17)) Listen and repeat the words and sounds.

/ɛr/	chair	
/ɪr/	ear	

b Put the words in the right place.

careful dear wear here they're
near stairs there we're hear where

c (4 18)) Listen and repeat the words.

d (4 19)) Listen and repeat. Copy the rhythm.

> A **Are** there any **stairs**?
> B **Yes**, they're **over there**.

> A **Is** there a **bank near here**?
> B **Yes**.
> A **Where**?
> B There's **one** in the **square**.

e Practice the dialogues with a partner.

f Ask your partner questions with *Is there a…in your…? Are there any…in your…?* Give more information in your answers if you can.

> TV books plants pictures
> mirror fireplace lamps
>
> kitchen bedroom bathroom
> dining room living room

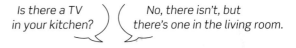

Is there a TV in your kitchen? No, there isn't, but there's one in the living room.

5 SPEAKING

a Look at the questionnaire **Your home**. Interview a partner. Ask for and give more information if you can.

Your home	
🏠 Do you live in a house or an apartment?	
🏠 How old is it?	
🏠 How big is it?	
🏠 How many	bedrooms are there? bathrooms?
🏠 Is there	a study? a yard or a balcony? a garage? heat or central air conditioning?
🏠 Do you like it? Why (not)?	

b Draw a simple plan of your living room. Show the plan to your partner and describe the room.

This is the living room. It's big and it's very light. There are two sofas and an armchair.

6 WRITING

➤ **p.114 Writing** *Describing your home.*
Write a description of your house or apartment.

7 (4 20)) SONG *House of the Rising Sun* ♫

G *there was / there were*
V prepositions: place and movement
P silent letters

Were there any pictures on the wall?

Yes, there was a picture of a lady.

8C A night in a haunted hotel

1 READING

a Do you believe in ghosts? Are there buildings in your town / city that people think are haunted?

b Read the text once and find out:

1 Who are the ghosts in the two hotels?

2 Check (✔) the things that happen in the hotels:

a ☐ people hear strange noises   d ☐ lights go on and off

b ☐ people see somebody   e ☐ things fall on the floor

c ☐ doors open and close   f ☐ people feel that somebody is watching them

c Look at the highlighted words in the text related to hotels and guess their meaning.

d Would you like to stay in one of these hotels? Why (not)?

WOULD YOU LIKE TO STAY IN A HAUNTED HOTEL?

THERE ARE MANY HOTELS IN BRITAIN THAT PEOPLE SAY ARE HAUNTED. IF YOU ARE FEELING BRAVE, YOU CAN STAY THE NIGHT IN ONE OF THESE HOTELS.

ENGLAND GOSFORTH HALL INN

Gosforth Hall is a small hotel in Cumbria in the north of England, built in 1658. People say the hotel has the ghost of a Catholic priest. He usually appears in Room 11. There is a secret tunnel that goes from behind the fireplace in the hotel lounge to Room 11. In 17th-century England, Catholic priests used the tunnel to hide from Protestants.

The owner of the hotel, Rod Davies, says, "I didn't believe in ghosts before I came here, but strange things happen in the hotel. One guest woke up in the middle of the night and saw a tall man standing next to his bed. He checked out the next morning." Rod's wife says, "One night a lot of books fell off a shelf in the lounge. And sometimes when I am working, I feel that someone is watching me, but when I turn around, nobody is there."

GHOST HUNTERS: Ask for Room 11   **www.gosforthhallhotel.co.uk**

SCOTLAND COMLONGON CASTLE

Comlongon is a 15th-century castle in a small village near Dumfries in southwest Scotland. The castle is haunted by the Green Lady, the ghost of Lady Marion Carruthers. Lady Marion was unhappy because she was married to a man she did not love, and in 1570 she jumped from the castle walls and killed herself. Many strange things happen in the hotel – doors open and close, and lights go on and off in empty rooms. An American couple once opened the door of their room and saw a young woman sitting on the bed. They left because they thought they were in the wrong room. In fact it was their room, but when they came back the room was empty.

GHOST HUNTERS: Ask for The Carruthers suite.   **www.comlongon.com**

2 VOCABULARY prepositions: place and movement

a Look at the pictures of the ghosts from the hotel. Where is the woman sitting? Where is the man standing?

b ➤ p.162 Vocabulary Bank *Prepositions: place and movement.*

3 PRONUNCIATION silent letters

> 🔍 **Silent letters**
> Some English words have a silent letter,
> e.g., in *cupboard* /ˈkʌbərd/ you don't pronounce the *p*.

a (4 23)) Listen and cross out the silent letter in these words.

> building   castle   could   friend   ghost   guest
> half   hour   know   listen   talk   what   write

b Practice saying the words.

4 LISTENING

A newspaper, the *Sunday Times*, sent one of its journalists, Stephen Bleach, to Gosforth Hall Inn. They asked him to spend the night in Room 11.

a (4 24)) Listen to **part 1** of Stephen's night. Correct the information in these sentences.

1 He arrived at Gosforth Hall early in the evening.

2 There were four other guests in the hotel.

3 He talked to one of the guests.

4 The manager was a man.

5 He went to his room at 11:00.

6 Room 11 was on the first floor.

7 The room was very small.

8 There was a TV and a remote control.

9 There was a horror movie on TV.

10 He went to sleep at the end of the movie.

b (4 25)) Do you think Stephen saw the ghost? Listen to **part 2** and find out. Listen again and answer the questions.

1 Did he wake up during the night?
  If yes, what time?

2 Did anything strange happen?
  If yes, what?

3 Did he "feel" the ghost?

4 Was he frightened?
  ☐ very   ☐ a little   ☐ not at all

5 Would he like to go back?
  Why (not)?

5 GRAMMAR
there was / there were

a (4 26)) Complete the sentences from the listening with *was*, *wasn't*, *were*, or *weren't*. Then listen and check.

1 There _____ many other guests in the hotel.

2 There _____ only three.

3 There _____ an old TV on a table.

4 There _____ a remote control.

b ➤ p.138 Grammar Bank 8C. Learn more about *there was / there were* and practice it.

6 SPEAKING

➤ **Communication** *The Ghost Room*
A *p104* B *p.109*. Look at the picture of another haunted hotel room for one minute. Try to remember what there was in the room.

Gosforth Hall Inn – Room 11

GRAMMAR

(Circle) a, b, or c.

1 Marilyn Monroe _____ an actress.
   a was   b were   c are
2 Where _____ Shakespeare born?
   a was   b were   c is
3 _____ the tickets expensive?
   a Was   b Were   c Did
4 I _____ a good movie on TV last night.
   a watched   b watch   c watches
5 They _____ at Stamford Bridge stadium.
   a didn't arrived
   b don't arrived
   c didn't arrive
6 _____ you see the soccer match last night?
   a Did   b Do   c Was
7 We _____ to Cuzco three years ago.
   a go   b were   c went
8 When _____ in Los Angeles?
   a you live
   b did you lived
   c did you live
9 I _____ you at the party last night.
   a didn't saw   b didn't see   c don't saw
10 What time _____ home?
    a did you get   b you did get   c you got
11 _____ a big table in the living room.
    a There are   b There is   c It is
12 How many bedrooms _____?
    a there are   b are there   c are they
13 There aren't _____ pictures on the walls.
    a any   b some   c a
14 _____ only three guests in the dining room.
    a There was   b There were   c There is
15 How many people _____ in the hotel?
    a there were
    b was there
    c were there

VOCABULARY

a Complete the professions with -er, -or, -ist, or -ian.
   1 act____   3 paint____   5 scient____
   2 art____   4 music____

b Complete the phrases with have, go, or get.
   1 _____ a good time   4 _____ a taxi
   2 _____ an email   5 _____ a sandwich
   3 _____ away for the weekend

c Complete the sentences with back, by, in, out, or to.
   1 I went _____ with my friends on Saturday night.
   2 They went home _____ car.
   3 What time did you get _____ the restaurant?
   4 I was born _____ 1982.
   5 After lunch, I went _____ to work.

d Label the pictures.

1 _____   2 _____   3 _____   4 _____   5 _____

e Write the prepositions.

1 _____   2 _____   3 _____   4 _____   5 _____

PRONUNCIATION

a (Circle) the word with a different sound.

   1 /ɪd/   wanted   waited   lived   ended
   2 [saw image]   saw   walked   thought could
   3 [egg image]   heard met   said   left
   4 [chair image]   near   there   wear   stairs
   5 [hat image]   hall   heat   hour   behind

b Underline the stressed syllable.

   1 mu|si|cian   2 a|go   3 yes|ter|day   4 be|tween   5 fire|place

CAN YOU UNDERSTAND THIS TEXT?

a Read the text and mark the sentences **T** (true) or **F** (false).

1 Arthur Conan Doyle was Scottish, but he worked in England.

2 He started writing stories about Sherlock Holmes while at university.

3 Conan Doyle lived at 221b Baker Street in London.

4 In 1893, he didn't want to write more Sherlock Holmes stories.

5 Sherlock Holmes didn't die in Austria.

6 Sherlock Holmes is very popular today.

b Look at the highlighted words or phrases in the text and guess their meaning.

The man who wrote
SHERLOCK HOLMES

Arthur Conan Doyle was born in Edinburgh on May 22, 1859. He studied medicine at Edinburgh University, and as a student, he began writing short stories. He became a doctor in the south of England, but at first, he didn't have many patients. So in his free time, he began writing stories about a very smart detective, Sherlock Holmes. Conan Doyle based Holmes's personality on one of his university professors. Holmes, who lives at 221b Baker Street in London, is famous for solving difficult crimes and mysteries using his great intelligence. The Sherlock Holmes stories soon became very popular, but in 1893, Conan Doyle became tired of his detective, and decided to "kill" him. In *The Final Problem*, Sherlock Holmes and his enemy, Professor Moriarty, die when they fall off the Reichenbach Falls in Switzerland. But people were very unhappy to lose Sherlock Holmes, and there were letters in many newspapers asking for him to come back. Finally, in 1901, Conan Doyle brought him back in a new story, *The Hound of the Baskervilles*. He explained that Holmes did not die in the Reichenbach Falls, but miraculously survived. Conan Doyle died on July 7, 1930, but Sherlock Holmes continues to live both in the stories and in many movie versions. Recently, he was the inspiration for the character Dr. Gregory House in the TV series *House*.

 CAN YOU UNDERSTAND THESE PEOPLE?
VIDEO

CAN YOU UNDERSTAND THESE PEOPLE?

(4 28)) **On the street** Watch or listen to five people and answer the questions.

Heba   Polly   Jeanna   Phoebe   Ben

1 Heba _____.
   a has family in New York
   b lives in Egypt
   c was born in Cairo

2 Polly went out for dinner on _____.
   a Friday   b Saturday   c Sunday

3 Jeanna likes her kitchen because _____.
   a it has a refrigerator
   b it's not big
   c it has two stoves

4 Phoebe's bedroom _____.
   a has a big bed
   b has nice windows
   c is big

5 Yesterday evening, Ben _____.
   a went out to a restaurant
   b worked at home
   c went to bed early

CAN YOU SAY THIS IN ENGLISH?

Do the tasks with a partner. Check (✓) the box if you can do them.

Can you…?

1 ☐ say three things about a famous (dead) person from your country

2 ☐ say five things you did last week, using past time expressions, e.g., last night, yesterday, (three) days ago, etc.

3 ☐ say where and when you were born

4 ☐ ask your partner five questions about yesterday

Short movies Edinburgh Castle
VIDEO Watch and enjoy the movie.

G countable / uncountable nouns; *a / an, some / any*
V food
P the letters *ea*

What did you have for lunch?

A pizza and some salad.

9A What I ate yesterday

1 VOCABULARY food

a What food words do you know in English? With a partner, try to think of five words.

b ▶ p.163 Vocabulary Bank *Food*.

2 READING

a Look at the photos that show meals that three people – a polo player, a model, and an actress – ate last week. Guess which person ate which meal.

b Read three articles from a series *New York Diet* in *New York Magazine*. Check your answers to **a**.

c Read the articles again. Answer the questions with **P** (the polo player), **M** (the model), or **A** (the actress). Who…?

1 never eats one kind of food?
2 didn't have salad for lunch?
3 has tea every morning?
4 didn't have soup for dinner?
5 had dinner at a restaurant?
6 didn't drink tea or coffee?
7 didn't eat any fruit?
8 had breakfast, lunch, and dinner in one place?
9 had home-cooked food?

d With a partner, look at the highlighted words related to food and guess their meaning. Use the photos to help you.

e Whose food do you prefer? Why?

1   2   3

What I ate last week

Nacho Figueras *polo player*

Wednesday

Breakfast   In the morning, I drank an Argentinian drink called *maté*. I put it in a pot, and I drink it with a straw. It's like green tea. I start every day with *maté*. I also had toast and cream cheese.

Lunch   I had a salad, just a regular salad at a hotel. I was in the area for a meeting, so I just had it there.

Dinner   We put the kids to sleep first. I kissed them good night. Then, I went to the Metropolitan Museum of Art restaurant with my wife. I had soup and a dish of mushroom risotto.

Selita Ebanks *model*

Sunday

Breakfast   I was in Dallas, Texas for business. I had a nice meal with my manager at the hotel. I had an omelet, toast, and pancakes. I also had coffee and orange juice.

Lunch   I had some meetings after breakfast, so I worked from the hotel. I had fruit, potato chips, and French fries sent to my room so I didn't have to leave the hotel.

Dinner   We ate in my manager's room. I had chicken and mashed potatoes. Then I flew from Dallas to New York City. The plane landed around 1 a.m. I drank a lot of water because I was so thirsty. When I got home, I had to walk my dogs!

Jennifer Esposito *actress*

Tuesday

Breakfast   I am very careful about what I eat. I don't eat food with wheat, or I get sick. I also don't eat at restaurants often. So I had a bowl of cereal with fruit for breakfast.

Lunch   Lunch was a big salad. I was at work on a new movie, so they got me a salad with olives, lettuce, carrots, and tomatoes.

Dinner   For dinner, I made soup with pasta and vegetables. I like to cook. About ten years ago when I was in Los Angeles, I was bored, so I started cooking to be creative.

> **risotto** an Italian dish made with rice and vegetable or meat broth
> **omelet** a dish with eggs, often with small pieces of meat, vegetables, or cheese
> **pancakes** thin, sweet, round cakes, cooked in a pan

3 GRAMMAR countable / uncountable nouns; a / an, some / any

a Look at the photos. Fill in the blanks with *a*, *an*, or *some*.

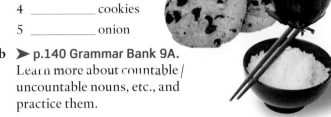

1 _____ strawberry
2 _____ tomato
3 _____ rice
4 _____ cookies
5 _____ onion

b ➤ **p.140 Grammar Bank 9A.** Learn more about countable / uncountable nouns, etc., and practice them.

c Make sentences with *there's a / an / some…* and *there are some…* Choose food and drink from **p.163 Vocabulary Bank** *Food*.

4 PRONUNCIATION the letters *ea*

a How is *ea* pronounced in these words? Put them in the correct column.

> bread breakfast eat healthy ice cream
> meat peas steak tea

🌳 tree	🥚 egg	🚂 train

b (4 31)) Listen and check. Practice saying the words. Which is the most common pronunciation of *ea*?

5 SPEAKING

a Make a food diary for yesterday. Write down what food and drink you had. Use **Vocabulary Bank** *Food p.163* to help you.

Breakfast *a cup of coffee, some cereal*

b Work in pairs. Tell each other what you had yesterday. Was it very similar or very different?

> *For breakfast, I had a cup of coffee and some cereal.*

6 LISTENING

a What cooking shows do you have on TV in your country? What do you think of them? Do you sometimes use their recipes?

b (4 32)) Listen to part 1 of a TV cooking competition called *Get ready! Cook!* where contestants have to cook an appetizer, a main course, and a dessert. Answer the questions.

1 How many ingredients are there in the bag?
2 How long do the contestants have to make their dishes?
3 Name *three* of the basic ingredients they can use.

c (4 33)) Listen to part 2. Complete the dishes that Jack and Liz make.

Jack	Judge's comments
1 _____ and _____ soup	
2 _____ breasts filled with cream _____	
3 pancakes with _____ sauce	

Liz	Judge's comments
1 carrot and _____ salad with _____ dressing	
2 _____ with creamy _____ sauce	
3 _____ and _____ mousse	

d ➤ **Communication** *Get ready! Cook! p.109* Look at the photos of their dishes. Whose dishes do you prefer?

e (4 34)) Listen to part 3. What does the judge say about Jack and Liz's dishes? Who wins?

f In pairs, think of one of your favorite dishes. Write the ingredients you need. Tell your partner.

G quantifiers: *how much / how many, a lot of*, etc.
V food containers
P /ʃ/ and /s/

> How much salt does it have?
>
> Not much.

9B White gold

1 VOCABULARY food containers

a (4 35)) Match the words and pictures. Listen and check.

☐ a <u>bottle</u>   ☐ a box   ☐ a can   ☐ a <u>car</u>ton   ☐ a jar   ☐ a <u>pack</u>age   ☐ a bag

b (4 36)) Listen and write five phrases.

c Make phrases with the containers and the words below.

> *a package of cookies*

cookies   chocolates   soda   potato chips   juice   jam   water   rice   sugar   tuna

2 GRAMMAR

quantifiers: *how much / how many, a lot of*, etc.

a Look at the pictures at the bottom of the page. Then ask and answer questions about the food.

a lot   a little / not much   none

> How much sugar is there in dark chocolate?
>
> I'm not sure. I think there's a lot.

b ► **Communication** *Sugar and salt p.109.* Check your answers to **a**.

c Complete the sentences with a food or drink from **a**.

1 There **isn't any** salt in _____.
2 There's **a little** sugar in _____.
3 There's **not much** salt in _____.
4 There's **a lot of** sugar in _____.

d ► **p.140 Grammar Bank 9B.** Learn more about quantifiers and practice them.

3 PRONUNCIATION /ʃ/ and /s/

a (4 38)) Listen and repeat the words and sounds.

ʃ		sugar fish	s		salt chocolates
shower			snake		

b (4 39)) Put the words in the right column. Listen and check.

cereal   sauce   delicious   fresh
information   center   rice   glass   reception
salad   science   shopping   special   sure

c (4 40)) Listen and repeat the dialogue. Then practice it with a partner.

A Are you sure this is salt? I think it's sugar.
B No, I'm sure it's salt. I put some in the rice salad.
A Let's taste the salad... Aargh. It was sugar. I told you.
B Sorry!

How much sugar?   How much salt?

4 SPEAKING

a Read the questionnaire and complete the questions with *How much* or *How many*.

> **How much sugar and salt do YOU have a day?**
>
> **Sugar**
> 1 _____ spoonfuls of sugar do you have in your tea or coffee?
>   **a** two or more   **b** one   **c** none
> 2 _____ cans of soda (or other carbonated drinks) do you drink a day?
>   **a** two or more   **b** one   **c** none
> 3 _____ fruit or fruit juice do you have a day?
>   **a** a lot   **b** not much   **c** none
> 4 _____ cookies do you eat a week?
>   **a** a lot   **b** not many   **c** none
>
> **Salt**
> 5 How often do you add salt to your food at the table?
>   **a** always   **b** sometimes   **c** never
> 6 _____ take-out food do you eat?
>   **a** a lot   **b** not much   **c** none
> 7 _____ bread do you eat a day?
>   **a** a lot   **b** a little   **c** none
> 8 _____ cheese do you eat a week?
>   **a** a lot   **b** a little   **c** none

b In pairs, interview your partner. Do you think he / she needs to eat less sugar and salt?

c Work in pairs. **A** say how much you eat / drink of the things below. **B** respond and ask for more information. Then say if you think **A** has a healthy diet or not. Change roles.

fish   meat   potatoes   vegetables   chocolate
fast food   eggs   pasta   olive oil   butter

I eat a lot of fish.   *How often do you eat fish?*

5 READING

a Read the magazine article *White Gold*. With a partner, complete the facts with *sugar* or *salt*.

b Read the article again, and highlight five new words or phrases. Compare with a partner.

c Did any of the facts surprise you?

6 ◀ 41 》 SONG *Sugar Sugar* ♫

WHITE GOLD
FASCINATING FACTS ABOUT SUGAR AND SALT

At different times in history, both sugar and salt were called "white gold," because they were so expensive and difficult to get. But there are many more interesting facts about sugar and salt…

- Christopher Columbus introduced [1]_____ to the New World in 1493 on his second voyage.

- If you eat too much [2]_____ (about .03 ounces per 2.2 pounds of weight), you can die. This was a method of ritual suicide in ancient China.

- Salzburg in Austria was called "the city of [3]_____" because of its mines.

- If you want to check if an egg is fresh, put it in a cup with water and [4]_____. If the egg floats, it isn't very fresh.

- In Brazil, fuel made from [5]_____ is used in cars instead of gas.

- Americans eat or drink about 5 pounds of [6]_____ a month.

- [7]_____ is used to make glass, laundry detergent, and paper.

- [8]_____ kills some bacteria, and so helps food to last longer, which is why cheese contains a lot.

- If you put [9]_____ into a vase of flowers, the flowers last longer.

- [10]_____ only contains energy. It doesn't contain any vitamins or minerals.

- *Sure* and [11]_____ are the only two words in the English language that begin with "su" and are pronounced "sh."

- We need to have a little [12]_____ in our diet, but not more than 4 grams a day, which is about one teaspoon.

G comparative adjectives
V high numbers
P /ər/, sentence stress

> Is the US bigger than Mexico?
>
> Yes, it's five times bigger.

9C Quiz night

1 VOCABULARY high numbers

a Read three questions from a radio quiz show. Choose the right answer for each question.

1 What is the approximate population of Vietnam?
   a 68,000,000
   b 78,000,000
   c 88,000,000

2 How many calories are there in a Big Mac?
   a 670
   b 540
   c 305

3 How far is it from New York City to Los Angeles?
   a about 2,500 miles
   b about 1,500 miles
   c about 3,100 miles

b (**4 42**))) Listen and check. How do you say the three answers?

c ▶ **p.148 Vocabulary Bank** *Days and numbers.* Do part 4.

d Look at the numbers below. Correct the mistakes.

175	a hundred and seventy-five
2,150	two thousand and one hundred and fifty
3,009	three thousand nine
20,000	twenty thousands
3,000,000	three millions

e (**4 44**))) Listen and write the ten numbers you hear.

f Answer the questions with a partner.
   1 What's the population of your town / city?
   2 What's the population of your country?
   3 How far is it from your town / city to…?
      a New York City
      b London

2 LISTENING

a (**4 45**))) What quiz shows are popular in your country? Listen to the introduction to a quiz show called *Quiz Night*. Answer the questions.

1 How long do the contestants have to say if the sentences are true or false?
2 How much do they win if they get…?
   a the first answer right _____   c the third answer right _____
   b the second answer right _____   d all eight answers right _____
3 If they get an answer wrong, how much do they lose?
4 What can a contestant do if they are not sure of the answer?

b In pairs, look at the sentences from *Quiz Night*. Write **T** (true) or **F** (false).

c (**4 46**))) Listen to a contestant on *Quiz Night*. Check your answers to **b**. How much does she win?

d Listen again for why the answers are true or false. Write down any numbers you hear.

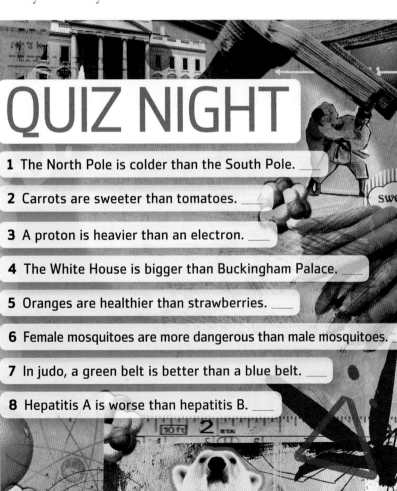

QUIZ NIGHT

1 The North Pole is colder than the South Pole. ___

2 Carrots are sweeter than tomatoes. ___

3 A proton is heavier than an electron. ___

4 The White House is bigger than Buckingham Palace. ___

5 Oranges are healthier than strawberries. ___

6 Female mosquitoes are more dangerous than male mosquitoes. ___

7 In judo, a green belt is better than a blue belt. ___

8 Hepatitis A is worse than hepatitis B. ___

3 GRAMMAR comparative adjectives

a Look at the adjectives in the quiz sentences. In pairs, answer the questions.

Using adjectives to compare two things:

1 What two letters do you put at the end of one-syllable adjectives (e.g., *cold*)?
2 Why is *big* different?
3 What happens when an adjective ends in *-y*?
4 What word do you put in front of long adjectives (e.g., *dangerous*)?
5 What's the comparative form of *good* and *bad*?
6 What's the missing word?
   China is bigger ___ Japan.

b ➤ p.140 Grammar Bank 9C. Learn more about comparative adjectives and practice them.

4 PRONUNCIATION

/ər/, sentence stress

a (4 48)》 Listen to the eight quiz sentences from **2**. How is *-er* pronounced at the end of a word?

b Listen again and repeat the sentences. Copy the <u>rhy</u>thm.

5 SPEAKING

➤ **Communication** *Quiz Night* **A** *p.105* **B** *p.110.* Play *Quiz Night.*

6 READING

a Read about three quiz shows. Do you have the same or similar shows in your country? Do you enjoy them?

b Now read about Ken Jennings. Why is he the best quiz contestant in the country?

c Read the article again and complete it with a verb from the list in the simple past.

answer ask be become get
give know play ~~win~~

d With a partner, look at the highlighted words in the texts related to quiz shows and guess their meaning.

e Would you like to be a contestant on a quiz show? Which one?

Jeopardy!

A quiz show where three contestants answer general knowledge questions about many different subjects. Correct answers must be in the form of a question. The contestant with the most money at the end wins.

Who Wants to Be a Millionaire?

A quiz show where contestants can win a maximum prize of one million dollars if they can answer multiple choice questions that become more and more difficult. Contestants can usually get help three ways: They can ask the audience, reduce the four choices to two, or call a friend.

Are You Smarter Than a 5th Grader?

A quiz show where contestants answer questions about subjects that 5th-grade students learn in school. If contestants need help, they ask actual 5th-grade students who are part of the show. When contestants give an incorrect answer or leave the game, they must say, "I'm not smarter than a 5th grader."

Q Who is the best quiz contestant in the country?

A Ken Jennings

In 2004, Ken Jennings, a 30-year-old software engineer, [1] <u>won</u> more games than anybody in US quiz show history. He [2]_____ a 74-game winner on *Jeopardy!* and won over $2.5 million!

But *Jeopardy!* [3]_____ not the only quiz show he appeared on. In 2008, Ken, competed on *Are You Smarter Than a 5th Grader?* He [4]_____ all the questions except the last one because he wasn't sure he [5]_____ the answer. He didn't win and had to say, "I'm not smarter than a 5th grader."

Ken was never a contestant on *Who Wants to Be a Millionaire?*, but he was an "expert"—a person with a lot of knowledge. When contestants needed help, they [6]_____ Ken.

In 2011, Ken [7]_____ *Jeopardy!* again. But this time he competed against past *Jeopardy!* champion Brad Rutter and Watson, an IBM supercomputer. In a two-game match, Watson beat both Ken and Brad. Ken was second and [8]_____ $300,000, which he [9]_____ to a charity.

1 🎥 AN INVITATION TO DINNER

a **(4 49)))** Watch or listen and mark the sentences **T** (true) or **F** (false).

1 Jenny and Rob worked last night.
2 Jenny wants to read Rob's article.
3 It's Eddie's birthday today.
4 Rob and Daniel invite Jenny to dinner.
5 Jenny says yes to Rob.

b Watch or listen again. Say why the **F** sentences are false.

c **(4 50)))** Read the information box. Listen and repeat **B**'s phrases.

🔍 **Responding to what somebody says**

1	**A** It's my birthday today.	**B**	Happy birthday!
2	**A** We won the game!	**B**	Congratulations!
3	**A** I have my driving test tomorrow.	**B**	Good luck!
4	**A** I got all my English homework right.	**B**	Good job!
5	**A** I didn't get the job.	**B**	Better luck next time.

d **(4 51)))** Listen and respond with phrases from the box.

))) *I got two goals this afternoon.* (*Good job!*

2 VOCABULARY
understanding a menu

a Complete the menu with **Main courses**, **Desserts**, or **Appetizers.**

b **(4 52)))** What do the highlighted words mean? How do you pronounce them? Listen and check.

c Cover the menu. In pairs, try to remember what's on the menu.

Luigi's

2 courses **$20.00**
3 courses **$29.00**

1 _____

Onion soup
Mozzarella and tomato salad

2 _____

Grilled chicken breast with vegetables
Mushroom ravioli
Seafood risotto

3 _____

Homemade vanilla ice cream with hot chocolate sauce
Fresh fruit salad
Tiramisu

3 ◼️ ORDERING A MEAL

a ④53))) Watch or listen to Jenny and Daniel having dinner. What food do they order?

b Watch or listen again. Complete the **You Hear** phrases.

))) You Hear	You Say 💬
Good evening. Do you have a _____ ?	Yes, a table for two. My name's Daniel O'Connor.
Come this _____, please.	
Are you ready to _____ ?	Yes. The soup and the mushroom ravioli, please. I'd like the mozzarella salad and then the chicken, please.
What would you _____ to drink?	Just water for me. A bottle of mineral water, please.
_____ or sparkling?	Is sparkling OK? Yes, sparkling.
Thank you, sir.	Thank you.

c ④54))) Watch or listen and repeat the **You Say** phrases. Copy the <u>rhythm</u>.

d Practice the dialogue in groups of three.

e 👥👥👥 In groups of three, role-play the dialogue. **A** is the waiter. Start with *Good evening. Do you have a reservation?* **B** and **C** go to *Luigi's.* Then change roles.

4 ◼️ THE END OF THE MEAL

a ④55))) Watch or listen and answer the questions.

1 How does Jenny usually celebrate her birthday?
2 Do they order dessert or coffee?
3 What does Daniel say to Jenny after the meal?
4 How does Jenny answer?
5 Does Barbara give Jenny good news or bad news?
6 Where does Jenny want to go after the meal?

b Look at the **Social English phrases**. Who says them: **J**enny, **D**aniel, the **w**aiter, or **B**arbara?

Social English phrases

Nothing special.	The same for me, please.
Would you like a dessert?	Go ahead.
Not for me, thanks.	Good news?
A decaf espresso.	Could I have the bill, please?

American and British English

check = American English   *bill* = British English

c ④56))) Watch or listen and check. Do you know what they are in your language?

d Watch or listen again and repeat the phrases.

👤 **Can you...?**
- [ ] use common phrases, e.g., *Good luck.*
- [ ] understand a menu
- [ ] order a meal

G superlative adjectives
V places and buildings
P consonant groups

> What's the oldest building in your town? I'm not sure. Probably the cathedral.

10A The most dangerous road...

1 VOCABULARY places and buildings

a Complete these famous tourist sights with a word from the list. Do you know what countries / cities they are in?

Bridge   Castle   Mountains   Square   Street

1 Trafalgar _____
2 The Golden Gate _____
3 Wall _____
4 Edinburgh _____
5 The Rocky _____

b (5 2)) Listen and check.

c ➤ p.164 **Vocabulary Bank** *Places and buildings.*

2 GRAMMAR superlative adjectives

a Look at the photos. Do you know what countries they are in?

b (5 4)) With a partner, complete the captions with a phrase from the list. Listen and check.

the biggest   the busiest   the most dangerous
the longest   the most popular   the widest

c Complete the chart with superlatives from **b**.

Adjective	Comparative	Superlative
big	bigger	*the biggest*
long	longer	
wide	wider	
busy	busier	
dangerous	more dangerous	
popular	more popular	

d What letters do you add to a one-syllable adjective to make a superlative? What words do you put before longer adjectives?

e ➤ p.142 **Grammar Bank 10A.** Learn more about superlative adjectives and practice them.

1 The Louvre is _____ art gallery in the world.

2 Vasco da Gama Bridge is _____ bridge in Europe.

3 The Yungas Road is _____ road in the world.

5 Avenida 9 de Julio in Buenos Aires is _____ street in the world.

4 Tiananmen Square is _____ square in the world.

6 Shinjuku Station in Tokyo is _____ train station in the world.

3 PRONUNCIATION consonant groups

a (5 6)) Listen and repeat the adjectives in **2c**.

> 🔍 **Consonant groups**
> Words that have two or three consonants together, e.g.,
> *fastest*, can be difficult to pronounce.

b (5 7)) Listen and repeat these superlatives.

the most expensive	the most exciting	the oldest
the most beautiful	the smallest	

c ➤ **Communication** *Cities quiz* **A** *p.105* **B** *p.110.*
Complete the questions with superlative adjectives.
Then ask and answer the questions with a partner.

4 READING

a Read the article below and look at the photo. Would
you like to ride a bike there? Why (not)?

b Read the article again. Then cover the text and answer
the questions in pairs.

1 Where is the North Yungas Road?
2 Why is it called "Death Road"?
3 How wide is the road?
4 Why is it popular with bike riders?
5 When is the most dangerous time of year to go?
6 Why is the road similar to London Bridge
and the Sydney Opera House?
7 Why didn't Marte enjoy riding a bike on the
Yungas Road?

c In pairs, guess the meaning of the highlighted words.

d Is riding a bike popular in your country / region? Is
there an area that is very popular with bike riders? Why?

5 SPEAKING & WRITING

a Work in pairs.

A Imagine you are a tourist in your town (or nearest big
town) who only speaks English. Ask **B**, who lives in
the town, questions 1–5. Get as much information
as you can.

B You live in your town. **A** is a tourist who doesn't speak
your language. Answer his / her questions (1–5).
Explain everything very clearly and give as much
information as you can!

Then change roles for questions 6–10.

What's the most beautiful park? — *I think Griffth Park.*

Where's that? — *It's downtown, near the Hollywood sign. It has...*

A		
1	What's _____ park?	(beautiful)
2	What's _____ way to get around?	(easy)
3	What's _____ museum?	(interesting)
4	What's _____ time of year to visit?	(good)
5	What's _____ place to eat typical food?	(nice)

B		
6	What's _____ building?	(old)
7	What's _____ place to go for a day trip?	(nice)
8	What's _____ area to walk at night?	(dangerous)
9	Where's _____ place to buy a souvenir?	(good)
10	What's _____ area to go at night?	(popular)

b Imagine you want to advertise your town / city for
tourists. Write an advertisement using superlative
adjectives. Add photos if you can.

*Come to Veracruz. It isn't the biggest or the most important
town in Mexico, but it has the nicest people and the most
delicious seafood...*

Riding a bike on the most dangerous road in the world

High in the Andes, the North Yungas Road goes from La Paz, the highest capital city in the world, to Coroico in the Yungas region of Bolivia. The road is only about ten feet wide and the Coroico River lies 656 feet below. Bolivians call it "El Camino de la Muerte" (Death Road) because of the number of accidents, and in 1995 it was officially declared "the most dangerous road in the world."

"One mistake and you are dead."

Since a new road opened in 2006, there are fewer buses and trucks on the old road. But now thousands of mountain bikers come from all over the world to take the most exciting ride of their lives. They start at La Cumbre, 15,400 feet above sea level, and go down to 5,000 feet, traveling at nearly 50 miles an hour down the narrow road. During the rainy season, from December to March, only experienced bike riders can take part, but some die every year on the road. So, why do people do it?

Andrew Jagoo, 26, from Melbourne, said after finishing the ride, "If you go to London, you have to see London Bridge, and if you go to Sydney, you have to see the Opera House, and if you go to Bolivia, you have to do the most dangerous road."

Marte Solberg, 22, from Norway said, "A lot of people said it was fun, but I was scared of falling down and dying. I was worried because I had no experience with mountain biking. One mistake and you are dead. I asked myself a thousand times, 'Why am I doing this?'"

G be going to (plans), future time expressions
V vacations
P sentence stress

What are you going to do? | I'm going to travel around the US.

10B CouchSurf around the world!

1 LISTENING

a Read the dictionary definition for *couch*, and look at the CouchSurfing website. What do you think CouchSurfing is?

> **couch** /kaʊtʃ/ *noun* **1** a long comfortable seat for two or more people to sit on (= a sofa) **2** the bed in a doctor's room for a patient to lie on

b (5 8)) Listen to part of a radio travel program. Were you right? How does CouchSurfing work?

c (5 9)) Now listen to the speaker give more details about CouchSurfing. Mark the sentences **T** (true) or **F** (false).

1 ☐ CouchSurfers usually pay their host a little money.
2 ☐ You need to create a profile on the website.
3 ☐ When you find a person with a bed, you call them to agree on the days you want to stay.
4 ☐ You have to offer other people a bed in your house or apartment.
5 ☐ CouchSurfing is safe because you can read what other travelers say about the host.
6 ☐ The host always shows their guests their city.
7 ☐ You can CouchSurf all over the world.

d Would you like to go CouchSurfing? Why (not)? Would you like to have a stranger stay in *your* house? Why (not)?

2 GRAMMAR *be going to* (plans)

a (5 10)) Iria González Liaño, a teacher from Spain, is going to CouchSurf through all 50 states in the US. Cover the dialogue and listen to the interview. What are her plans?

Listen again and fill in the blanks with a verb.

Host Tell me about your plans, Iria.
Iria I'm going to ¹ *travel* around the US – to all 50 states.
Host Wow! That's amazing! How long are you going to ² _____ in each state?
Iria I'm not sure, but I think maybe three nights in each state—maybe more in big states like California and Texas.
Host Who are you going to ³ _____ with?
Iria I'm going to stay with all kinds of people. I want to make new friends across the US!
Host Are you going to ⁴ _____ on a couch?
Iria Yes, I'm going to sleep on a lot of couches!
Host How are you going to ⁵ _____?
Iria I'm going to ⁶ _____ mostly by bus.
Host What are you going to ⁷ _____ in each state?
Iria I don't just want to see the typical tourist sights. I hope I'm going to ⁸ _____ things that aren't in a guide book.
Host Well, have a good trip and good luck!

c Look at the **highlighted** sentences in the dialogue. Then answer the questions.

1 What form is the verb after *going to*?
2 Do we use *going to* to talk about the past, the present, or the future?

d ➤ **p.142 Grammar Bank 10B.** Learn more about *be going to* (plans) and practice it.

e Number the future time expressions 1–8.

☐ tonight   ☐ tomorrow night
☐ next year   1 today
☐ tomorrow morning ☐ next week
☐ next month   ☐ tomorrow afternoon

f (5 12)) Listen and check. Then listen again and repeat. Make four true sentences about your plans.

3 PRONUNCIATION & SPEAKING
sentence stress

a **5 13**)) Listen and repeat the highlighted phrases in **2b**. Copy the <u>rhythm</u>.

I'm **going** to <u>travel</u> around the <u>US.</u>

b ➤ **Communication** *What are you going to do?* **A** p.105 **B** p.110. Interview a partner about his / her plans.

4 READING

a Read Iria's blog about her CouchSurfing trip. Did she have a good time?

b Read the blog again. Then cover it and answer the questions from memory.

  1 What color was the desert in New Mexico?
  2 Where were the big, beautiful houses?
  3 Which state didn't have much to do?
  4 What information did she have in case things didn't work out?
  5 What was a problem she had?
  6 How did she feel before meeting a host?

c Read the blog again and look at the highlighted verb phrases. With a partner, say what you think they mean.

 I had fun CouchSurfing through the US. Every state had something interesting to see. In my opinion, the best states were New Mexico and Rhode Island. I loved the desert and its pretty, brown colors in New Mexico. I also enjoyed the Spanish history there. In Rhode Island, I took a tour of some big, beautiful houses. North Dakota was my least favorite state because there wasn't much to do.

I never had a bad experience while CouchSurfing. However, I always had a hotel address in case things didn't work out. I met all kinds of people, and I slept in all kinds of places, from comfortable beds to old couches! I only had one problem—sometimes I arrived late at a host's house. Once it was because I forgot to change the time on my watch. Another time I got lost. Then one time I didn't have a cell phone, so I couldn't call my host and my host couldn't call me! Whenever that happened, I tried to stay calm. CouchSurfers and hosts are usually friendly and very understanding.

 The best thing about CouchSurfing is seeing the world and meeting new people at the same time. I love that when I travel somewhere, I have "friends" to stay with. I'm always excited before meeting a host. And the worst thing about CouchSurfing? Sometimes the couch you sleep on can be very surprising. That's the real adventure!

5 VOCABULARY & SPEAKING
vocations

a Complete the vacation phrases using a verb from the list.

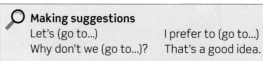

go have see stay show

  1 _____ in a hotel / with a friend / for a week
  2 _____ somebody around your town / city
  3 _____ the sights
  4 _____ by train (bus, plane) / back home
  5 _____ a good time / nice meals

b In pairs, plan a vacation. You are going to visit **three** cities on the same continent. Your vacation can be a maximum of **ten** days.

  Answer the questions:

  • What cities are you going to visit?
  • Where are you going to stay?
  • How are you going to get there?
  • How long are you going to stay in each city?
  • What are you going to do in each place?

> 🔍 **Making suggestions**
> Let's (go to...)   I prefer to (go to...)
> Why don't we (go to...)? That's a good idea.

c Change partners. Tell each other about your vacation plans.

> *We're going to go to South America – to Buenos Aires, Rio, and Montevideo. We're going to CouchSurf because we don't have much money...*

d Do you prefer your new partner's plans? Would you like to change partners and go with him / her?

6 WRITING

➤ **p.115 Writing** *A formal email.* Make a reservation at a Bed and Breakfast.

G *be going to* (predictions)
V verb phrases
P the letters *oo*

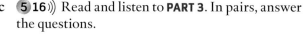

Am I going to fall in love? Yes, and you're going to be very happy.

10C What's going to happen?

1 VOCABULARY verb phrases

a Do people in your country go to fortune-tellers, or use fortune-telling sites on the Internet? Do *you* believe in fortune-telling?

b Match the fortune-teller's cards and verb phrases.

☐ become <u>fa</u>mous	☐ get a lot of <u>mo</u>ney
☐ get a new job	☐ have a sur<u>prise</u>
☐ get <u>mar</u>ried	A be <u>luck</u>y
☐ meet <u>some</u>body new	☐ <u>trav</u>el
☐ fall in love	☐ move to a new house

2 READING & LISTENING

a (5 14)) Read and listen to **PART 1** of a story. In pairs, answer the questions.

1 Who does Jane want to see?
2 Who is going to tell her about her future? Why?
3 Why couldn't she see the man very well?

b (5 15)) Listen to part 2. Then, with a partner, complete the information.

1 Jane has a problem with her _____.
2 She chooses _____ cards.
3 Her first card means she's going to be _____.
4 Jane asks the fortune-teller if she's going to _____ with her boyfriend.

c (5 16)) Read and listen to **PART 3**. In pairs, answer the questions.

1 What's the second card? What does it mean?
2 Why is this a problem for Jane?
3 What's her third card? What does it mean?
4 Who's Jim? Where did Jane meet him?
5 What do you think the fourth card is going to be?

d (5 17)) Listen to part 4. Then, with a partner, complete the information.

1 Her fourth card means she is going to _____ her boyfriend and go away with Jim to _____.
2 Very soon they are going to _____.
3 Jane asks if she is going to be _____ and the fortune-teller says _____.
4 She pays the fortune-teller $_____.

e (5 18)) Read and listen to **PART 5**. In pairs, answer the questions.

1 Who was the fortune-teller?
2 Why did he pay Madame Yolanda $100?
3 What's the fifth card? What do you think is going to happen?

It's written in the cards

PART 1

"Come in," said a voice. Jane Ross opened the door and went into a small room. There was a man sitting behind a table.

"Good afternoon," said Jane.

"I want to see Madame Yolanda, the fortune-teller."

"Madame Yolanda isn't here today," said the man. "But don't worry. I'm going to tell you about your future. What questions do you want to ask?" Jane looked at the fortune-teller. She couldn't see him very well because the room was very dark.

PART 3

He turned over the second card.

"Hmm, a house. A new house. You're going to move, very soon, to another country."

"But my boyfriend works here. He can't move to another country."

"Let's look at the next card," said the fortune-teller. He turned over the third card.

"A heart. You're going to fall in love."

"With who?" asked Jane.

"Let me concentrate. I can see a tall man. He's very attractive."

"Oh, that's Jim," said Jane.

"Who's Jim? Your boyfriend?"

"No. Jim's a man I met at a party last month. He's an actor, from New York. He says he's in love with me. It was his idea for me to come to Madame Yolanda."

"Well, the card says that you're going to fall in love with him."

"Are you sure?" asked Jane. "But what about my boyfriend?"

"Let's look at the fourth card," said the fortune-teller.

PART 5

The fortune-teller stood up. He turned on the light. At that moment, an old woman came in. "So, what happened?" she asked.

"It was perfect! She believed everything," said Jim. "I told you, I'm a very good actor. She was sure I was a fortune-teller!"

He gave the woman $100.

"That's Jane's $50 and another $50 from me. Thanks very much, Madame Yolanda. Bye."

Madame Yolanda took the money. The fifth card was still on the table, facedown. She turned it over. It was the plane. She looked at it for a minute and then she shouted:

"Wait, young man! Don't travel with that girl – her plane is going to..."

But the room was empty.

3 GRAMMAR be going to (predictions)

a Look at these two sentences. Which one is a <u>plan</u>? Which one is a <u>prediction</u>?

1 She's going to be very lucky.

2 She's going to go on vacation next week.

b ▶ p.142 Grammar Bank 10C. Learn more about *be going to* (predictions) and practice it.

c Write four predictions, about the **weather**, **sports**, **your town** / **country**, and **you**. Use *I think…going to…*

I think it's going to snow tonight.

d Compare your predictions with a partner. Do you agree?

4 PRONUNCIATION the letters *oo*

> 🔍 **The pronunciation of *oo***
> *oo* can be pronounced /ʊ/ (e.g., *book* /bʊk/) or /u/ (e.g., *spoon* /spun/). Use your dictionary to check the pronunciation of new *oo* words.
> Be careful, *room* can be pronounced /rʊm/ or /rum/.

a (5 20)) Listen to the two sound words. Can you hear the difference in the vowel sound?

🐂 bull		👢 boot

b (5 21)) Listen and write the words in the right column.

afternoon   book   choose   cook   food   good
look   moon   school   soon   spoon   too   took

c (5 22)) Listen and check.

d Practice saying the sentences.

Good afternoon.   *It's too soon!*
Look at the moon!   *Is the food good?*
He's a good-looking cook.

5 SPEAKING

Role-play fortune-telling.

A Look at the ten cards in **1**. Secretly, number the cards 1–10 in a different order.

B Choose five numbers between 1 and 10.

A Predict **B**'s future using those cards.

B Ask for more information. Then change roles.

A *I'm going to tell you about your future. Your first card is a star. You're going to become famous. You're going to be on TV...*

B *Great! What show?*

6 (5 23)) SONG *Fortune Teller* ♫

GRAMMAR

(Circle) a, b, or c.

1 There's _____ milk in the refrigerator.
   a some b any c a

2 We don't need _____ bread.
   a no b any c a

3 How _____ fruit do you eat a day?
   a much b many c a lot

4 I drink _____ coffee.
   a much b a lot c a lot of

5 **A** How much salt do you eat?
   B _____.
   a A little b A few c Much

6 **A** Is there any sugar?
   B No, sorry, _____.
   a there isn't none
   b there isn't any
   c there isn't some

7 Tea is _____ coffee in this cafe.
   a cheaper that
   b more cheap than
   c cheaper than

8 Oranges are _____ than bananas.
   a more healthy b healthier c healthyer

9 My English is _____ than my brother's.
   a gooder b better c more good

10 This is _____ size that we have.
   a the biggest b the most big c the bigger

11 It's _____ restaurant in the city.
   a the baddest b the worst c the worse

12 What's _____ park in your town?
   a the most beautiful
   b most beautiful
   c the more beautiful

13 _____ to buy my ticket this afternoon.
   a I go b I going c I'm going

14 _____ to get married?
   a Do they going
   b They are going
   c Are they going

15 I think _____ tomorrow.
   a it snows
   b it's snowing
   c it's going to snow

VOCABULARY

a (Circle) the word that is different.

1 breakfast   lunch   dessert   dinner
2 strawberries   mushrooms   onions   peas
3 orange juice   sugar   milk   water
4 potato chips   French fries   tomatoes   potatoes
5 fruit salad   ice cream   cake   chicken

b Match the food and the containers.

   soda fruit juice cookies sugar honey

1 a can of _____   3 a jar of _____   5 a carton of _____
2 a bag of _____   4 a package of _____

c (Circle) the right word or phrase.

1 It's *a hundred twenty | a hundred and twenty* miles from here.
2 The population is about three *million | millions*.
3 That new *department mall | department store* is great.
4 Let's have a snack at one of those cafes in the *square | bridge*.
5 Where is the main train *office | station*?

d Complete the phrases with these verbs.

   become fall get go have meet move see show stay

1 _____ in a hotel   6 _____ the sights in a city
2 _____ by bus   7 _____ somebody new
3 _____ famous   8 _____ somebody around your city
4 _____ married   9 _____ a great meal
5 _____ in love   10 _____ to a new house

PRONUNCIATION

a (Circle) the word with a different sound.

1   bread   peas   meat   tea

2   sugar   shopping   fish   soda

3   cereal   carrots   salad   rice

4   chef   church   chicken   cheese

5   food   cook   book   good

b Underline the stressed syllable.

1 cho|co|late   3 su|per|mar|ket   5 dan|ge|rous
2 de|ssert   4 in|te|res|ting

CAN YOU UNDERSTAND THIS TEXT?

a Read the article once. Then read it again and choose a, b, or c.

1 A survey showed that Americans _____.
   a eat 15 percent more junk food than healthy food
   b eat the same amount of junk food as healthy food
   c eat too much junk food

2 Americans have unhealthy diets because _____.
   a they eat cheap food
   b they think healthy foods are expensive
   c they think cooking at home is expensive

3 Americans can make their diets better, if they _____.
   a spend a lot of money
   b cook more often at home
   c never eat fast food

b Look at the highlighted words or phrases in the text and guess their meaning.

The unhealthy American diet

The US has a problem with obesity, and the government says we need to have healthier diets. However, American shoppers are continuing to fill their supermarket baskets with unhealthy food.

A survey showed that more than 30 percent of calories Americans eat comes from junk food—food high in salt, sugar, and fat. And nearly 15 percent of Americans eat a fast-food meal every day (e.g., a hamburger, French fries, and a soda).

Children have a problem, too. Scientists say that children born today can die before their parents because of obesity and unhealthy food choices by their families.

Why do Americans have unhealthy diets? There are many reasons, but money is the main one. Americans think that healthy foods are more expensive than packaged foods. They also think it takes a long time to cook a healthy meal.

So, how can Americans make their diets better? They can stop eating fast food and cook more often at home. They can bring healthy lunches to work or school, and they can have fruit for snacks during the day.

VIDEO CAN YOU UNDERSTAND THESE PEOPLE?

5 24)) **On the street** Watch or listen to five people and answer the questions.

Yvonne   Cecile   Joel   Reed   Arja

1 Yvonne doesn't eat much _____.
   a fruit   b sugar   c salt

2 Cecile cooks excellent _____ food.
   a Italian   b Indian   c Indonesian

3 Joel likes Barcelona because there are a lot of _____.
   a great stores   b great buildings   c great beaches

4 Reed is going to stay at his _____'s house in Los Angeles.
   a aunt   b friend   c family

5 When Arja compares the US to her country she doesn't mention _____.
   a the food   b the buildings   c the weather

CAN YOU SAY THIS IN ENGLISH?

Do the tasks with a partner. Check (✓) the box if you can do them.

Can you...?

1 ☐ say what you usually have for breakfast

2 ☐ compare your country with the US in three ways

3 ☐ ask your partner four questions with the superlative of the **bold** adjective
   • What's _____ present you've ever bought? **expensive**
   • What's _____ movie you've seen this year? **good**
   • What's _____ vacation you've ever had? **bad**
   • What's _____ place you've ever been to? **cold**

4 ☐ ask your partner what he / she is going to do
   • tonight   • tomorrow   • next weekend

 Short movies the history of the sandwich
VIDEO Watch and enjoy the movie.

G adverbs (manner and modifiers)
V common adverbs
P word stress

11A First impressions

How do they dress? They dress very fashionably, but casually.

1 READING

a Look at the photos of three cities. Do you know what countries they are in?

Atlanta

Malmö

Valencia

b Read two blogs on a travel website, about people's first impressions of two of these cities. Which two are they?

c Read the blogs again. Answer with the names of the cities.

Where...?

1 do people eat a lot of salt and sugar
2 do TV shows have subtitles
3 are the days very short in winter
4 do a lot of people have bad habits when they drive
5 is the city safer than the writer thought
6 are the houses colorfully painted
7 do you see men taking care of young children
8 do people speak very slowly

Travel blogs

September 16

Kate in _____

The driving

I think people drive really dangerously, which surprised me because I thought they were careful drivers here. They don't drive fast, but people are always on the phone in the car, which you don't see much in my country nowadays.

The food

The food can be delicious, but I think people eat very unhealthily. In restaurants, they often add salt to their food. And they drink a lot of soda! The headquarters of the Coca-Cola company is based here, and they even have a Coca-Cola museum. Once I went to a coffee shop and asked for a double espresso, no milk and no sugar. I had to repeat my order three times because the waitress couldn't understand me. She said people here only ask for lattes and cappuccinos with a lot of sugar!

The people

In general, people are very friendly. The people I'm staying with, who live just outside the city, know all their neighbors really well. They often don't lock their doors, which surprised me because people say it's a dangerous city. They speak incredibly slowly, with a strong accent and sometimes I have a problem understanding them.

December 14

Mark in _____

The weather

It's December and it gets dark at about 3 p.m., which is depressing! There's a lot of snow right now, but all the buses and trains are running perfectly, not like in my country where everything stops when it snows!

The houses

All the houses are painted in pretty colors, like red, green, and blue. And many houses have a yellow and blue flag. Inside, the houses are decorated beautifully with a lot of flowers and modern wooden furniture.

The people

People are friendly and polite, but formal. They dress fashionably but casually, and of course, you see a lot of very blond women here. You also see a lot of men who are taking care of very young babies. Everybody speaks English really well, maybe because a lot of the TV is in English with subtitles.

d Find words in the blogs that mean:

Kate

Para 1	_____	*adv*	at this time
Para 2	_____	*noun*	the office where the leaders of an organization work
Para 3	_____	*verb*	close with a key

Mark

Para 4	_____	*adj*	sth making you feel sad
Para 5	_____	*adj*	made from a tree
Para 6	_____	*adv*	not in a formal way

e Which of the two cities would you prefer to live in? Why?

2 GRAMMAR adverbs

a Look at the highlighted adverbs in the blogs. Answer the questions.

1 What two letters are added to an adjective to make an adverb?
2 Which adverb is the same word as the adjective?
3 Which is the adverb from *good*?
4 Which three adverbs are describing other adverbs?

b Now look at the highlighted adverbs again in Kate's first paragraph. Complete the rules with *before* or *after*.

1 Some adverbs describe how people do things.
They go _____ the verb or verb phrase.
2 Some adverbs describe another adverb (or adjective).
They go _____ the adverb (or adjective).

c ➤ **p.144 Grammar Bank 11A.** Learn more about adverbs and practice them.

d ⑤27))) Listen and say what is happening. Use an adverb.

They're speaking quietly.

3 PRONUNCIATION word stress

a Underline the stressed syllable in the adjectives.

Adjectives	Adverbs
dan|ge|rous	dangerously
po|lite	politely
beau|ti|ful	beautifully
in|cre|di|ble	incredibly
care|ful	carefully
fa|shio|na|ble	fashionably
ca|su|al	casually
per|fect	perfectly
un|heal|thy	unhealthily

b ⑤28))) Listen and check. Repeat the adjectives.

c ⑤29))) Now listen and repeat the adverbs. Does the stress change?

4 LISTENING & SPEAKING

a ⑤30))) Listen to Jemma talking about the third city. In general, is she positive, negative, or neutral about it?

b Listen again. Then, with a partner, complete Jemma's sentences.

Eating out
People spend a lot of time in ¹_____. People who ²_____ go out to have ³_____. They don't have it in their ⁴_____.
When people go out in big groups, ⁵_____ _____ all sit at one end of the table and ⁶_____ _____ at the other.

The women
Women here talk very ⁷_____ and very ⁸_____.
Women dress ⁹_____ _____.

Work
There's a myth that the Spanish don't ¹⁰_____ _____, but I don't think it's ¹¹_____.
People have a ¹²_____ lunch break, but they leave work very ¹³_____.

c Answer the questions in small groups.

1 In your country or city how do people...?
• dress for special occasions
• treat tourists
• drive
• eat at lunchtime during the week
• speak foreign languages
• behave during sports games
• decorate their houses

2 Think of a time when you went to another country or another city / region in your country for the first time. What did you notice about...?
• the people
• the food
• the driving
• the houses
• the weather

5 WRITING

Choose two headings from the blogs in **1** or the listening in **4**. Write two paragraphs, either about your country or a country you have visited.

G verbs + infinitive
V verbs that take the infinitive
P sentence stress

Would you like
to get a new job?

No, I want to
stay where I am.

11B What do you want to do?

1 READING & SPEAKING

a Read about the website 43things.com.
How does it work?

> **43Things** is a website where
> people write things that they want to do.
> There are always 43 different ambitions.
> Some are trivial, and some are more serious.
> Other people respond and write about their
> experiences and sometimes give advice.

b Read today's 43 things and responses A–E.
Match the responses with five things people
want to do. Do you think their advice is good?

c Complete the phrases from the text with a
verb from the list.

---
be<u>come</u> bite choose climb /klaɪm/
<u>down</u>load go learn spend <u>v</u>isit
---

1 _____ a mountain
2 _____ on a safari
3 _____ to cook
4 _____ less time on the Internet
5 _____ the lyrics
6 _____ five things you really like eating
7 _____ a Goth
8 _____ all the continents
9 _____ my nails

d Cover the verbs and try to remember them.

2 GRAMMAR verbs + infinitive

a Look at the highlighted verbs in the text.
What's the form of the next verb? Which
one is different?

b ➤ **p.144 Grammar Bank 11B.** Learn more
about verbs + infinitive and practice them.

What do **you** want to do with your life?

On 43Things today, people want to...

climb Mount Kilimanjaro   get up earlier   **go on a safari**
get a new job   have very long hair   **have more time for myself**
learn to cook   learn to dance like Shakira   **make a short movie**
visit all the continents   spend less time on the Internet   write a novel
read 12 books a month   run a half marathon   see Radiohead live
learn to speak Italian   stop biting my nails   **get married**
go to Iceland   write a song   **become a Goth**   paint my kitchen
spend less money on clothes   **stop eating meat**   stay awake for 24 hours

A Spend less time on Facebook, for example, only two
hours on weekends. Stop using Second Life if you use
it. (I uninstalled it.)

B Get a Laura Pausini CD. Download the lyrics to a song
and translate them – you can use Google Translate for
this. Listen carefully to the pronunciation, and then
sing along with her. (I sang "Incancellabile.")

C You just need to stop cutting it! Don't worry about the
latest fashions. Go for it!

D Choose five things you really like eating (e.g., roast
chicken and chocolate cake) and then look at recipes
on the Internet. Choose the recipes that you'd like to
try, preferably ones that aren't too difficult. Make the
five things again and again until they're perfect. It isn't
difficult. You just need to practice.

E Wear black clothes. Be yourself, and listen to bands like
The Cult and The Mission.

Second Life® a website that is a free 3D virtual world where users
can socialize, create new personalities, and interact with other users
Laura Pausini an Italian pop singer, popular in several European and
Latin American countries

3 PRONUNCIATION sentence stress

a (5 32)) Listen and repeat the dialogue. Copy the <u>rhy</u>thm. How do you pronounce *to*?

> **A** **Would** you **like** to **go** to **Iceland**?
> **B** **No**, I **wouldn't**.
> **A** **Why not**?
> **B** **Because** I **don't like** the **cold**.

b (5 33)) Listen to another dialogue. Complete the missing stressed words.

> **A** _____ you _____ to _____ a _____ _____?
> **B** _____, I'd _____ to.
> **A** _____?
> **B** Because I _____ my _____. It's _____ _____.

c Practice the dialogues with a partner.

d In pairs, choose ten ambitions from **What do you want to do with your life?** Ask your partner questions using *Would you like to...?*

> *Would you like to climb Mount Kilimanjaro?* *Yes, I would. / No, I wouldn't.*

4 SPEAKING

Work in pairs. Take turns.
A Tell your partner about the things below.
B Respond to what **A** says. Ask questions.
A Ask *What about you?*

> ➲ a country you **want to go** to
> ➲ something you **would like to learn to do**
> ➲ something you **need to do** tomorrow
> ➲ a vacation you **are planning to take** soon
> ➲ a famous person **you hope to meet** one day
> ➲ a movie you **want to see** soon
> ➲ a dangerous sport **you would like to try**
> ➲ something you **need to buy** soon
> ➲ a singer or group you **hope to see** one day

> *I really want to go to Australia.* *Oh, yes? Why Australia?*

5 WRITING

a Create a class page for **43Things**. Write three things you really want to do. Your teacher will write some of them on the board.

b Read other students' ambitions and choose one that you know something about. Write a response (like the ones in **43Things**) to give advice or talk about your experience.

6 (5 34)) SONG *Don't Tell Me that it's Over* ♫

Do men and women use the Internet in the same way?

No, they don't. They're very different.

11C Men, women, and the Internet

1 VOCABULARY & PRONUNCIATION
the Internet

a Do you ever visit any of the websites on this page, or websites like them? How much time do you spend a day on the Internet? Do you use it mainly for your work / studies or for pleasure?

b Look at some words and phrases related to the Internet. Match them with their definitions.

a|ttach|ment   down|load   goo|gle   log in   on|line
search for   skype   so|cial net|work   up|load   wi|fi

1	_____	*adj, adv* on the Internet
2	_____	*noun* sth you send with an email, e.g., a document or a photo
3	_____	*verb* to move sth from your computer to an Internet site, e.g., photos
4	_____	*verb* to move sth from an Internet site to your computer, e.g., music, movies
5	_____	*verb* to type words into the search engine *Google®* to find information about sb / sth
6	_____	*verb* to make a telephone call over the Internet
7	_____	*verb* to type your username (usually your name or email address) and a password to begin using a computer or a website
8	_____	*noun* a way of connecting a computer to the Internet without wires
9	_____	*noun* a website that people use to communicate, e.g., *Facebook*, *Twitter*, etc.
10	_____	*verb* to try to find sb or sth, e.g., on the Internet

Dictionary abbreviations
sth = something   **sb** = somebody

c **5 35))** Listen and check. Repeat the words. <u>Un</u>derline the stressed syllable in the multisyllable words.

2 SPEAKING & LISTENING

a With a partner, look at some things that people do on the Internet. For each one, say if you do it often, sometimes, hardly ever, or never.

> *I often send emails for work. What about you?*

- [ ] send personal emails
- [ ] send emails for work
- [ ] read the news
- [ ] buy things on shopping websites
- [ ] buy things on *eBay* (or a similar site)
- [ ] get sports information
- [ ] visit websites about health and medicine
- [ ] use social networks
- [ ] play games
- [ ] download music
- [ ] visit forums about diet or caring for children
- [ ] use online banking
- [ ] use online maps for directions
- [ ] book tickets and hotels online

b Now go through the list again and write **M** if you think men do them <u>more</u> than women, **W** if you think women do them <u>more</u> than men, and **ND** if you think there is no difference.

c (5 36)) Listen to an interview with a marketing expert about how men and women use the Internet. Check your answers.

d Do you think the situation is the same in your country?

3 GRAMMAR articles

a Complete the email with *a*, *an*, *the*, or – (= no article).

Sent: Friday, July 8 4:16 PM
To: Carola Whitney
Subject: **Re: Hello!**

Hi Carola,

Thanks for your email. I would really like to write to you and practice my English.

I'm ¹_____ student at Buenos Aires University. It's ²_____ biggest university in Argentina. I'm studying ³_____ medicine. I live in Buenos Aires with my grandmother, ⁴_____ my mother's mother, because my family lives in ⁵_____ small town far away, but I go ⁶____ home on ⁷_____ weekend.

I love listening to ⁸_____ classical music, and ⁹_____ last week, I went to ¹⁰_____ amazing concert at ¹¹_____ Opera House here.

---

b ➤ p.144 Grammar Bank 11C. Learn more about articles and practice them.

c Work in pairs. **A** choose a circle. Think of three things, three places, etc., and tell **B**. **B** respond and ask for more information. Then change roles.

> *I love fish, strawberries, and chocolate cake. I don't like tomatoes.*

> *Tomatoes? Why not?*

3 kinds of food you love (and one you don't like)

3 things you sometimes do on Saturday evening

3 things you always have in your bag or pocket

3 things you do first thing in the morning

3 things you did last night

3 things women usually like doing (but men don't)

3 jobs you would like to do (and one you wouldn't)

3 things men usually like doing (but women don't)

1 🎥 JENNY'S LAST MORNING

a (5 38))) Watch or listen and mark the sentences **T** (true) or **F** (false).

1 Rob arrives late.
2 He has a coffee with Jenny.
3 Jenny has good news for him.
4 The job offer is for a year.
5 Rob thinks *A Writer in New York* is a good name for the column.
6 Rob needs time to think.

b Watch or listen again. Say why the **F** sentences are false.

2 VOCABULARY public transportation

a Match the words and pictures.

4	train
	plane
	taxi
	bus
	ferry
	subway

b (5 39))) Listen and check.

c Complete the headings with a word from **a**.

1 _____
You get one at a stand or by waving your hand.
They are also called cabs.
People usually give the driver a tip (= some extra money, about 10–20%).
In New York City, they are yellow.

2 _____
You get one at an airport.
First, you have to check in.
Then you go through security to the departure lounge.
Finally, you go to your gate.

3 _____
You get one at a station.
You usually need to buy a ticket or card first.
Then you need to find the right platform.
Most go underground in big cities.

4 _____
You get one at a station or a stop.
Some are public and some are private.
You can buy a ticket in advance or sometimes you can pay the driver.
In New York City, they are white and blue.

d Cover the columns and look at the headings. Try to remember the four facts about each type of public transportation.

3 ◧ GETTING TO THE AIRPORT

a (5 40)») Watch or listen to Jenny's three conversations. How does she get to the airport?

b Watch or listen again. Complete the **You Hear** phrases.

You Say 💬	))) You Hear
Could you call me a taxi, please?	Yes, of course. _____ to?
To Paddington station.	And when would you like it _____?
Now, please.	
How much is it?	That's £_____, please.
Make it £15. And could I have a receipt?	Thank you very much, _____.
Could I have a ticket to Heathrow Airport, please?	Single or _____?
Single, please.	Standard or _____ class?
Standard, please.	That's £18.
Can I pay by credit card?	Yes, of _____.

c (5 41)») Watch or listen and repeat the **You Say** phrases. Copy the <u>rhythm</u>.

d Practice the dialogue with a partner.

e 👥 In pairs, role-play the dialogue. Then change roles.

A (book open) You are the receptionist, the taxi driver, and the ticket clerk. The taxi costs $12.60. The ticket costs $32.50.

B (book closed) You want to get a taxi to Penn Station, and then a train to JFK Airport. Begin with *Could you call me a taxi, please?*

4 ◧ SAYING GOODBYE

a (5 42)») Watch or listen and answer the questions.

1 What does Jenny leave in the hotel?
2 How does she get it back?
3 What has Rob decided to do?
4 Is Eddie going to meet her at the airport? Why (not)?
5 Who is Eddie? How old is he?

b Look at the **Social English phrases**. Who says them: **J**enny or **R**ob?

Social English phrases	American and British English
I can't believe it!	*one-way ticket* = American English
Thank you so much.	*single ticket* = British English
I'd love to [accept].	*round-trip ticket* = American English
I'm so happy.	*return ticket* = British English
Have a good journey.	*coach* = American English
See you in [New York].	*standard* = British English

c (5 43)») Watch or listen and check. How do you say them in your language?

d Watch or listen again and repeat the phrases.

> 👤 **Can you...?**
> ☐ ask for a taxi
> ☐ buy a ticket for public transportation
> ☐ use common phrases, e.g., *Thank you so much*, *See you in New York*, etc.

G present perfect
V irregular past participles
P sentence stress

12A Books and movies

Have you seen the movie?

No, I haven't, but I've read the book.

1 GRAMMAR present perfect

a Look at some images from movies. What do the movies have in common?

b (5 44)) Listen to Alan and Lucy talking on the phone. What two things are they going to do tonight?

c Listen again and read the conversation. Complete the chart below and answer the questions with a partner.

Alan	Hi, Lucy. Have you finished your report?
Lucy	Yes, I have, finally!
Alan	What do you want to do tonight? Do you want to go out?
Lucy	No, I'm a little tired.
Alan	Would you like to come here? I can order pizza and we can watch a movie.
Lucy	Good idea. What movies do you have?
Alan	How about *Eclipse*? Have you seen it?
Lucy	No, I haven't seen it, but I've read the book.
Alan	Is it good?
Lucy	I loved it! Vampires – perfect for a winter night!
Alan	Great. What pizza topping do you want?
Lucy	Cheese and blood, please...no, cheese and tomato.

+	I've seen the movie.
–	I _____ the movie.
?	_____ you _____ the movie?

1 What is *'ve*? What verb is *seen* from?

2 Change the three sentences in the chart to third person singular (*He* or *She*).

3 Lucy says, *"I've read the book."* Do we know *when* she read it?

d ➤ **p.146 Grammar Bank 12A.** Learn more about the present perfect and practice it.

e Look at the movies in **a** and talk to a partner. Which of the movies have you seen? Have you read any of the books?

I've seen Eclipse, but I haven't read the book.

I haven't seen the movie of Alice in Wonderland, but I've read the book.

The Lord of the Rings

Eclipse

The Hunger Games

Alice in Wonderland

2 PRONUNCIATION sentence stress

a (5 46)) Listen and repeat the dialogue. <u>C</u>opy the <u>rhy</u>thm.

A **Have** you **seen** *The Hobbit*?
B **No**, I **haven't**.
A **Have** you **read** the **book**?
B **Yes**, I **have**. I've **read** it **twice**.

b Write down the names of three more movies from books. Ask and answer with a partner.

Have you seen...?
Have you read the book?

Yes, I have. /
No, I haven't.

3 VOCABULARY
irregular past participles

a Look at some irregular past participles. Which verbs do you think they are from? Write the base form and the simple past.

	base form	simple past	past participle
1	*be*	*was / were*	been
2			broken
3			done
4			eaten
5			fallen
6			forgotten
7			gone
8			left
9			sung
10			spoken
11			taken
12			worn

b (5 47)) Listen and check.

c (5 48)) Cover **a**. Listen and say the simple past and past participle.

)) *be* (*was / were, been*

d Complete the **Verb** column with a past participle from **a**.

Verb

1 Have you ▨ your homework? ____
2 I'm sorry, I've ▨ your name. ____
3 Have you ever ▨ a photo of an actor? ____
4 Ann's ▨ on vacation. She's going to be away for three weeks. ____
5 Have you ▨ to Mike about the party? ____
6 I've never ▨ that jacket. It was a big mistake. ____
7 Jim's ▨ in love with an Argentinian woman. ____
8 Oh, no! I've ▨ my glasses. ____

e Cover the **Verb** column. Can you remember the sentences?

4 SPEAKING & LISTENING

a Complete the phrases with the past participle of the verb in parentheses.

MOVIE EXPERIENCES
Find someone who has...

		Name	What movie was it?
1	_____ asleep watching a movie (fall)		
2	_____ the soundtrack of a movie (buy)		
3	_____ the movie theater before the end of a movie (leave)		
4	_____ a movie more than three times (see)		
5	_____ during a movie (cry)		
6	_____ a movie in English with subtitles (see)		
7	_____ in a movie (appear)		

b Stand up and move around the class. Ask *Have you ever…?* questions with 1–7. When somebody answers *Yes, I have*, write down his or her name and ask *What movie was it?*

c (5 49)) Listen to three people answering one of the questions from **a**. Which question is it?

d Listen again. Complete the chart for each person.

	Which movie?	How many?	Why?
1			
2			
3			

5 (5 50)) SONG *Flashdance* ♫

G present perfect or simple past?
V more irregular past participles
P irregular past participles

Have you been to New York City? Yes, I have. I went there last year.

12B I've never been there!

1 LISTENING

a Are you following a TV series right now? Which one? Why do you like it?

b (5 51)) Look at the information about an episode from an American TV series. Listen to part of the episode. Then answer questions 1 and 2.

▶ ⏮ 0:00.00 / 0:27:35

Episode 5
Jess's birthday is on Friday and Matt wants to take her somewhere special...

1 Which restaurants has Jess eaten at before? Check (✓) or put an ✗ in the boxes.

☐ The Peking Duck ☐ Appetito ☐ Luigi's

2 Do they agree on which restaurant to go to?

c Listen again and answer the questions.

1 When did Jess go to *The Peking Duck* and who with?
2 How many times has she been to *Appetito*?
3 What did Matt say happened when they went to *Luigi's*?
4 Why is Jess angry?
5 Who does Jess think Matt went with to *Luigi's*?
6 What does Matt say? Do you believe him?

2 GRAMMAR
present perfect or simple past?

a Look at part of the conversation between Matt and Jess. In pairs, answer the questions.

> **Matt** Have you been to *The Peking Duck*?
> **Jess** Yes, I have.
> **Matt** Oh, no! When did you go there?
> **Jess** Last month. I went with some people from work.

1 What tense is Matt's first question?
2 What tense is Matt's second question?
3 Which of the two questions is about a specific time in the past?

b ➤ **p.146 Grammar Bank 12B.** Learn more about the present perfect and simple past and practice them.

c Play *Guess where I've been.*

Guess where I've been

1 Write down the names of **six** cities in your country or abroad (three you **have been to** and three you **haven't been to.**)

2 Exchange lists with your partner. Check (✓) the three cities you think your partner has been to, but don't tell him / her.

3 Ask *Have you been to...?* for each place to check your guesses. Did you guess correctly?

(*Have you been to Boston?*

4 Now ask some simple past questions for the cities your partner *has* been to.

(*When did you go to...?*

(*Did you like it?*

---

3 VOCABULARY & PRONUNCIATION
more irregular past participles

a Look at some more irregular past participles. Write the base form and the simple past.

1	_buy_	_bought_	bought
2	_____	_____	drunk
3	_____	_____	found
4	_____	_____	given
5	_____	_____	heard
6	_____	_____	had
7	_____	_____	known
8	_____	_____	lost
9	_____	_____	made
10	_____	_____	met
11	_____	_____	paid
12	_____	_____	sent
13	_____	_____	spent
14	_____	_____	thought
15	_____	_____	won

b (5 54)) Listen and check.

c ➤ **p.165 Irregular verbs** Check (✓) all the ones you know. Try to learn the new ones.

d (5 55)) Put three irregular past participles in each column. Listen and check.

bought	broken	cost	done	driven
drunk	forgotten	given	gone	got
known	lost	made	paid	spoken
sung	taken	written		

clock	fish	train

up	phone	saw

e Play past participle *Bingo*.

4 SPEAKING

a Look at question 1 below. What words are missing in the present perfect question? What words are missing in the simple past question? What form do you need of the verb in **bold**?

Recently...

Present perfect	Simple past
1 / **be** to the movie theater recently?	What / see? / like it?
2 / **buy** any new clothes recently?	What / buy?
3 / **have** a really good meal recently?	Where / go? What / have?
4 / **be** to a sports event recently?	/ your team win?

In your life...

Present perfect	Simple past
5 / ever **be** on TV?	What TV show / it?
6 / ever **lose** your cell phone?	Where / lose it? / find it?
7 / ever **win** a cup or medal?	What / win it for?
8 / ever **speak** to a famous person?	Who / it? What / say?

b Work in pairs. **A** ask **B** the questions. If **B** answers *Yes, I have*, ask the simple past questions, too. Then change roles.

G review: question formation
V review: word groups
P review: sounds

12C The *American English File* questionnaire

1 READING

a Read the information about Sir Ian McKellen. Have you seen any of his movies? Did you like them?

> **Sir Ian McKellen** is one of Britain's greatest actors. He was born in Burnley in the north of England on May 25, 1939. He first became well known as an actor for his roles in Shakespeare's plays, e.g., *Hamlet* and *Macbeth*. In recent years, he has had many important movie roles including James Whale in *Gods and Monsters*, Gandalf in *The Lord of the Rings* trilogy, and Magneto in *X-Men*.

b Sir Ian McKellen agreed to be interviewed especially for *American English File*. Read the interview and write a heading from the list below in each section.

YOUR ABILITIES

YOUR WORK EXPERIENCES

YOUR HOME

YOUR LIFESTYLE

YOUR PLACES

YOUR TASTES

c Read the interview again. Then mark the sentences **T** (true) or **F** (false). Say why the **F** ones are false.

1 He became an actor when he was a student.
2 He lives outside London.
3 He gets up early every day.
4 He's never been to India.
5 He spends a long time on the Internet every day.
6 He read *The Lord of the Rings* when he was young.
7 His desk isn't very neat.
8 He doesn't like animals.
9 He relaxes by playing games.
10 He doesn't have any ambitions.

INTERVIEW WITH SIR IAN MCKELLEN

1 *YOUR TASTES*

What kind of music do you like?
I hardly ever listen to music at home – I prefer going to concerts. I enjoy classical music and pop, but my favorite kind of music is traditional American jazz.

What book are you reading right now?
I'm reading *The Hammersteins*, a biography of the American theater family written by Oscar Andrew Hammerstein.

Who's your favorite historical character?
Perhaps William Shakespeare.

2

What time do you usually get up in the morning?
If I am working, I get up one hour before I have to leave the house. If I am not working, and I went to bed late the night before, I get up at about 10 in the morning.

How much time do you spend a day on the Internet?
I can very easily spend three or four hours on the Internet, answering emails, reading the news, etc. I think of the Internet as a wonderful encyclopedia of information.

How do you relax?
I enjoy a late night sudoku, but especially being with friends.

3

What's your favorite room in the house?
Perhaps the living room where I cook and eat, and from where I can see the River Thames in London.

What do you always have on your desk?
I always have too many letters, papers, and books which are waiting for me to read.

Do you have any pets? I love dogs, but I can't have one because I'm often away from home.

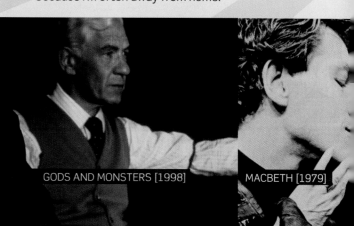

X-MEN [2000]

GODS AND MONSTERS [1998]

MACBETH [1979]

4

What languages do you speak?
I only speak English, but I can remember a little of the French I learned at school.

Can you play a musical instrument? No.

Is there something you would like to learn to do? Yes – many things, e.g., to sing well, to play the piano, and to speak foreign languages.

5

What's your favorite place in London?
I love the River Thames and the views from its many bridges.

Where are you going to go for your next vacation? I'm going to go to India for the first time in February.

What's the most beautiful city you've ever visited? I can't choose between Edinburgh, Prague, and Venice.

6

What was your first job?
The first money I earned as a professional actor was when I was a student at Cambridge University in 1959. I played small parts in audio recordings of Shakespeare's plays.

When did you first read *The Lord of the Rings*?
I read it first when I was preparing to play Gandalf in the movie trilogy.

What was the best and worst thing about filming *The Lord of the Rings*?
The best thing about filming was discovering the countryside and people of New Zealand. But the worst thing was living away from home for a year or more.

LORD OF THE RINGS [2003]

2 VOCABULARY review: word groups

a Put these words from the interview in the right column.

| actor | books | desk | go to bed | living room | small |

Rooms	Things	Jobs

Furniture	Adjectives	Daily routine

b With a partner, add three more words to each column.

3 PRONUNCIATION review: sounds

a Look at some words from the interview. Which word has a different sound?

1 school   choose   cook   too

2 first   earn   worst   year

3 say   wait   can't   favorite

4 friends   many   people   ever

5 enjoy   bridge   dog   languages

6 hour   home   perhaps   hardly

7 thing   three   the   think

8 information   school   traditional   professional

b (5 56))) Listen and check. Practice saying the words.

4 GRAMMAR & SPEAKING
review: question formation

a Without looking back at the interview, try to remember the questions for these answers.

1 Perhaps William Shakespeare.
2 I'm going to go to India for the first time in February.
3 I only speak English…
4 I can't choose between Edinburgh, Prague, and Venice.
5 I read it first when I was preparing to play Gandalf…

b Choose eight questions from the questionnaire to ask a partner.

GRAMMAR

(Circle) a, b, or c.

1 You speak _____.
  a very slow
  b very slowly
  c very slower

2 She plays tennis _____.
  a really well
  b really good
  c really goodly

3 My husband works _____.
  a incredible hard
  b incredibly hard
  c incredibly hardly

4 I'd like _____ a Ferrari.
  a drive   b to drive   c driving

5 What do we need _____ next?
  a to do   b do   c doing

6 She wants to pass her exams, but she doesn't like _____.
  a study   b studing   c studying

7 _____ usually drive fast in this country.
  a The men   b Men   c The man

8 I saw _____ good movie last night.
  a the   b a   c –

9 It's _____ best place to eat in the city.
  a the   b a   c –

10 Do you go to _____ bed late on weekends?
  a the   b a   c –

11 I've read the book, but I _____ the movie.
  a don't see
  b haven't saw
  c haven't seen

12 A Have you _____ anyone famous?
   B Yes, I have. A famous movie actor.
  a ever met   b ever meet   c met ever

13 _____ he been to New York?
  a Has   b Did   c Have

14 We _____ to Canada last year.
  a have gone   b have been   c went

15 She _____ in a restaurant before.
  a did never worked
  b have never worked
  c has never worked

VOCABULARY

a Write the opposite adjective or adverb.

1 quickly _____   3 well _____   5 formal _____
2 safe _____   4 noisy _____   6 healthily _____

b Complete the sentences with these verbs.

need   learn   promise   want

1 I'd like to _____ to dance the tango.
2 You don't _____ to wash it. You've only worn it once.
3 I can't _____ to be on time. It depends on the traffic.
4 Do you _____ to go to a restaurant or to a cafe for lunch?

c Complete the sentences with these Internet words.

attachment   wifi   download   online   website

1 I do a lot of shopping _____ these days.
2 I can _____ the song for you tonight.
3 You can find all the information on the hotel's _____.
4 Don't open an _____ when you don't know who it's from.
5 We have _____ at home so I can send emails from my bedroom.

d Complete the sentences with *for*, *in*, *with*, or *up*.

1 Log _____ with your username and password.
2 I looked _____ *U2* on Wikipedia – they started in 1976.
3 You can search _____ all kinds of information on the Internet.
4 Have you ever seen a movie _____ subtitles?

e Write the past participle of the following verbs.

1 see saw _____   3 know knew _____   5 fall fell _____
2 go went _____   4 give gave _____   6 take took _____

PRONUNCIATION

a (Circle) the word with a different sound.

1 [↑]   done   sung   gone   won

2 [ɛ]   said   been   any   left

3 [æ]   want   had   father   watch

4 [u]   choose   soon   food   book

5 [ɜr]   worst   wore   prefer   search

b Underline the stressed syllable.

1 po|lite|ly   2 dan|ge|rous|ly   3 de|cide   4 a|ttach|ment   5 web|site

CAN YOU UNDERSTAND THIS TEXT?

a Read the text and mark the sentences **T** (true) or **F** (false).

1 It is more expensive to live in the US than in the UK.
2 It is less expensive to be sick in the UK.
3 Waiters are better in UK restaurants.
4 It's more difficult to make friends in the US.
5 Americans are more direct than the British.

b Look at the highlighted words or phrases in the text and guess their meaning.

Amy Johnson is an English woman who lives and works in the US. We asked her to tell us about her first impressions of the US.

One of my first impressions was that the US is cheaper than the UK. I live in Ohio and the cost of living (rent, bills food, etc.) is lower than in Oxford, where I'm from in the UK. The only thing that's more expensive here is healthcare. You need to have health insurance, which can be very expensive. Of course in the UK, it's free to go to the doctor's or to the hospital.

Eating out is less expensive in the US as well and the service is better, but you can eat very well in England. There's a wide variety of food from all around the world (Chinese, Japanese, Italian, Turkish, etc.). And generally, I'd say British food is healthier than American food, and the portions are a lot smaller, too.

As for the people, I find Americans very positive and optimistic about the future compared to British people, who can be pessimistic. Also, when I'm in Ohio, I talk to everybody: salespeople, the person behind me in the supermarket line, the person sitting next to me in the restaurant. I can't do that in the UK – people are much more reserved. But, on the other hand, I think it's easier to make real friends in the UK than in the US.

I also think British people are not very good at telling you what they really think or (in a work situation) saying something negative about you. Americans just say things as they are!

VIDEO CAN YOU UNDERSTAND THESE PEOPLE?

5 57))) On the street Watch or listen to five people and answer the questions.

Arja   James   Ruth   Ben   Justin

1 Arja is visiting the US for _____.
  a a month
  b four days
  c for the first time
2 James would like to _____.
  a have a beautiful garden
  b build a great park
  c be a gardener in a park
3 When Ruth talks about *Mamma Mia*, she doesn't mention _____.
  a the actors b the soundtrack c the story
4 Ben thinks that women drive _____ than men.
  a more slowly b less dangerously c better
5 Justin went to a karaoke bar _____.
  a a long time ago b quite recently c last year

CAN YOU SAY THIS IN ENGLISH?

Do the tasks with a partner. Check (✓) the box if you can do them.

Can you...?
1 ☐ say how people in your country a) drive b) dress
2 ☐ say three things you would like to do in the future
3 ☐ say which of the following you prefer and why
  • classical music or pop music
  • summer vacations or winter vacations
  • Chinese food or Japanese food
4 ☐ say what things you do on the Internet and how often
5 ☐ answer the questions below
  • What city have you been to recently?
  • When did you go there?
  • What did you do there?
  • What's the best / worst thing about your town?

> **VIDEO Short movies** historic theater
> Watch and enjoy the movie.

Communication

7A WHERE WERE YOU? Student A

a Ask **B** your questions. Ask *Where were you at…?*

- 9 o'clock yesterday morning
- 11:30 yesterday evening
- 3 o'clock yesterday afternoon
- 12 o'clock last night
- 6:30 yesterday evening
- 7 o'clock this morning

b Answer **B**'s questions.

> **Useful language**
> **at** home / work / school
> **in** bed / the library / my car / college
> **on** the bus / the train / the street

7B STAMFORD BRIDGE Students A+B

Tourist Information
STAMFORD BRIDGE

Stamford Bridge is a small village in the North of England, near York. It is about 230 miles (370 kilometers) from London. It has a population of 3,500 people. It is famous for a battle between the English and the Vikings in 1066.

NOTE: Don't confuse Stamford Bridge near York with Stamford Bridge in London, the stadium of Chelsea Football Club!

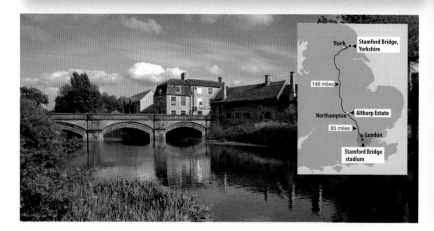

7C A NIGHT TO REMEMBER Student A

a Ask **B** the questions about Mehmet's night.

> 1 When and where was it? (*Last year, in Istanbul.*)
> 2 Who was he with? Why? (*His friends. It was his best friend's birthday.*)
> 3 What color T-shirt did he wear? (*Black.*)
> 4 What is Cezayir? (*It's an old building with a restaurant.*)
> 5 What did they do after dinner? (*They had some coffee and then they went to the beach to swim.*)
> 6 Was the water cold? (*No, it was warm.*)
> 7 Why did he go home in his friend's car? (*Because he couldn't find his car keys.*)
> 8 What time did he get home? (*Really late, at five o'clock in the morning.*)

b Answer **B**'s questions about Maggie's night.

c Whose memory is better?

8A POLICE INTERVIEW
Student A

Work in pairs with another **A**. You are police officers. There was a robbery last night. **B** and **B** are two friends. You think they were responsible. They say that they went out for dinner and went to the movies last night. You want to know if this is true.

a Look at the police interview form and prepare to ask the **B**s the questions. Think of more questions to get more details about the evening, e.g., *What did you wear? What did you eat and drink? What movie was it?*

b Interview one of the **B**s. Write down his / her answers in the form. (Your partner interviews the other **B**.)

c Compare with your partner. Did the two **B**s tell exactly the same story? If not, arrest them!

POLICE INTERVIEW FORM

Name: _____ Date: _____

	What time?	Where?	More details:
/ meet?			
/ have dinner?			
/ go to the movies?			

What / do after the movies?	
What time / get home?	

8C THE GHOST ROOM Student A

a Look at the picture for a minute. Try to remember what's in the room.

b Ask **B** the questions.

- / a TV? (*No, there wasn't.*)
- / a double or a single bed? (*There was a single bed.*)
- / a mirror? Where was it? (*Yes, there was. It was on the table.*)
- / any plants? (*No, there weren't.*)
- / any books in the room? (*No, there weren't.*)
- How many windows / ? (*There were two.*)

c Close your books. Answer **B**'s questions.

Communication

9C QUIZ NIGHT Student A

a Complete your sentences 1–8 with the comparative of the **bold** adjectives.

> 1 **small** Brazil is _____ than the US.
> (*True. Brazil is 3.3 million square miles and the US is 3.79 million square miles.*)
>
> 2 **long** The Amazon River is _____ than the Nile River.
> (*False. The Amazon is about 4,000 miles long and the Nile is about 4,130 miles long.*)
>
> 3 **old** Oxford University is _____ than Cambridge University.
> (*True. Oxford University was founded in 1167 and Cambridge 43 years later.*)
>
> 4 **short** The English alphabet is _____ than the Arabic alphabet.
> (*True. There are 26 letters in the English alphabet and 28 in the Arabic alphabet.*)
>
> 5 **dangerous** K2 is _____ to climb than Mount Everest.
> (*True. 25% of climbers who get to the top of K2 die, but only 9% of climbers of Everest die.*)
>
> 6 **large** A gigabyte is _____ than a megabyte.
> (*True. A megabyte is 1,000 bytes, but a gigabyte is 1,000 megabytes.*)
>
> 7 **dry** The Sahara Desert is _____ than the Atacama Desert.
> (*False. Sahara Desert average rainfall = 0.79 inches; Atacama Desert average rainfall = 0.004 inches.*)
>
> 8 **far** New Zealand is _____ south than Australia.
> (*True. It's about 1,242 miles southeast of Australia.*)

b Play *Quiz Night*. You are the host.

> • Read your sentence 1 to **B**. **B** says if it's true or false.
> • Tell **B** if he / she is right and give the extra information in parentheses.
> • If **B** is right, he / she wins 500 dollars. Then read sentence 2 for 1,000 dollars, sentence 3 for 2,000 dollars, sentence 4 for 4,000 dollars, etc.
> • If **B** gets a question wrong, he / she loses the money, but continues to play. The prize starts again from 500 dollars.

c Play *Quiz Night* again. You are the contestant.

10A CITIES QUIZ Student A

a Complete your questions with the superlative of the adjectives in parentheses.

> 1 What's the _____ city in the world? (noisy)
> a **Tokyo** b Madrid c Santiago
>
> 2 What's the _____ city in the world? (hot)
> a Rio de Janeiro b **Bangkok** c Nairobi
>
> 3 Which city has the _____ monument in the world? (popular)
> a New York b **Paris** c Istanbul
>
> 4 What's the _____ city in the US? (wet)
> a Chicago b San Diego c **New Orleans**
>
> 5 Which city has the _____ traffic jams in the world? (bad)
> a São Paulo b **Beijing** c Mexico City

b Answer **B**'s questions.

c Ask **B** your questions. Does he / she know the answers? (The correct answers are in **bold**.)

> *What's the noisiest city in the world—Tokyo, Madrid, or Santiago?*

10B WHAT ARE YOU GOING TO DO?
Student A

a Ask **B** the questions below.

Tonight	• What / do tonight? • / study English? Why (not)?
Tomorrow	• What time / get up tomorrow? • Where / have lunch?
Next weekend	• / go away next weekend? Where to? • What / do on Saturday night?

b Answer **B**'s questions.

7A WHERE WERE YOU? Student B

a Answer **A**'s questions.

> **A** *Where were you at nine o'clock yesterday morning?* **B** *I was in bed.*

b Ask **A** your questions. Ask *Where were you at…?*

- 8:30 yesterday morning
- 6:30 yesterday evening
- 11:30 yesterday morning
- 10 o'clock last night
- 5 o'clock yesterday afternoon
- 6:30 this morning

> **Useful language**
> **at** home / work / school
> **in** bed / the library / my car / college
> **on** the bus / the train / the street

7C A NIGHT TO REMEMBER Student B

a Answer **A**'s questions about Mehmet's night.

b Ask **A** the questions about Maggie's night.

> 1 Where was she with her family? (*In New York City.*)
> 2 Who did she want to see? (*Her favorite actor, Nick Jonas.*)
> 3 Who got the tickets for the Broadway show? (*Her father got the tickets.*)
> 4 What color coat did she wear? (*Red*)
> 5 Who opened the door for them? (*A theater worker.*)
> 6 Why was she excited? (*Because Nick Jonas spoke to her.*)
> 7 What else happened? (*Nick took some pictures with them and wished her sister a happy birthday.*)
> 8 What was the weather like? (*It was a cold, cloudy night*).
> 9 What time did she get back to the hotel? (*At eleven o'clock in the evening.*)

c Whose memory is better?

8A POLICE INTERVIEW Student B

Work in pairs with another **B**. You are friends. Last night you met, had dinner, and went to the movies. There was a robbery last night. **A** and **A** are police officers. They think you were responsible, and they want to interview you separately. If you both tell the same story, you are innocent!

a Prepare your story. Use these questions. Think of extra details, e.g., *What did you wear? What did you eat and drink? What movie was it?*

- What time / where did you meet?
- What time / where did you have dinner?
- What time / where did you go to the movies?
- What did you do after the movies?
- What time did you get home?

b Answer **A**'s questions.

c Did you and your friend tell the same story?

Communication

8C THE GHOST ROOM Student B

a Look at the picture for a minute. Try to remember what's in the room.

b Close your books. Answer **A**'s questions.

c Ask **A** the questions.

- / a clock? Where was it?
  (*Yes, there was. It was next to the window.*)
- / a rug on the floor? (*No, there wasn't.*)
- / a lamp or light? Where was it?
  (*Yes, there was. It was on the wall.*)
- / any pictures on the wall? What of?
  (*Yes, there was one. It was of a woman.*)
- / any cupboards? (*No, there weren't.*)
- How many chairs / ? (*There was one.*)

9A GET READY! COOK! Students A+B

Jack's Meal

Appetizer

carrot and orange soup

Main course

chicken breasts filled with cream cheese

Dessert

pancakes with chocolate sauce

Liz's Meal

Appetizer

carrot and onion salad

Main course

pasta with creamy chicken sauce

Dessert

chocolate and orange mousse

9B SUGAR AND SALT
Students A+B

How much sugar?

According to the American Heart Association, a woman should have no more than 20g (grams) of sugar a day (= 5 teaspoons) and a man no more than 36g (= 9 teaspoons).

- a can of Coke has approximately 39g of sugar
- an apple has approximately 23g of sugar
- a small (40g) bar of dark chocolate has approximately 7g of sugar
- an egg doesn't have any sugar

How much salt?

According to UK Government studies, an adult should eat no more than 6g of salt a day.

- a small bag of potato chips has approximately .15g of salt
- a slice of white bread has approximately 0.5g of salt
- a bottle of water has approximately 0.0023g of salt
- a bottle of olive oil doesn't have any salt

9C QUIZ NIGHT Student B

a Complete your sentences 1–8 with the comparative of the **bold** adjectives.

1 **old** The pyramids in Egypt are _____ than the Parthenon in Greece.
(*True. The pyramids are about 4,500 years old and the Parthenon is about 2,500 years old.*)

2 **short** World War I was _____ than World War II.
(*True. World War I lasted four years (1914–1918), but World War II lasted six years (1939–1945).*)

3 **high** The mountains on Earth are _____ than the mountains on Mars.
(*False. Olympus Mons on Mars is 16 miles high; Everest is about 5 miles high.*)

4 **big** China is _____ than Canada.
(*False. Canada is about 3,800,000 square miles; China is about 3,700,000 square miles.*)

5 **popular** Coffee is _____ with women than men in the US.
(*False. On average, men drink 1.9 cups of coffee a day and women drink 1.4 cups of coffee a day.*)

6 **warm** The Mediterranean Sea is _____ than the Red Sea.
(*False. Mediterranean Sea average temperature = 75–78 °F; Red Sea average = 78–86 °F.*)

7 **good** It's _____ to do exercise in the morning than in the afternoon.
(*False. In the afternoon between 4 and 5 p.m., the body temperature is at its maximum, which means it is the perfect time to exercise.*)

8 **hot** The earth is _____ than the moon.
(*False. The average temperature of the moon is about 225 °F during the day; the average temperature of the earth is 55–62 °F.*)

b Play *Quiz Night*. You are the contestant.

- **A** will read you his / her sentence 1. You say if it's true or false.
- **A** will tell you if you are right, and give you extra information.
- If you are right, you win 500 dollars. **A** then reads you sentence 2 for 1,000 dollars, sentence 3 for 2,000 dollars, sentence 4 for 4,000 dollars, etc.
- If you get a question wrong, you lose all the money, but continue to play. The prize starts again from 500 dollars.

c Play *Quiz Night* again. You are the host. Use your questions 1–8.

10A CITIES QUIZ Student B

a Complete your questions with the superlative of the adjectives in parentheses.

b Ask **A** your questions. Does he / she know the answers? (the correct answers are in **bold**.)

1 Which city has the _____ quality of life in the world? (good)
   a Tokyo   b **Copenhagen**   c Miami

2 Which US city has the _____ population? (big)
   a **New York**   b Chicago   c San Francisco

3 Which city has the _____ airport in the world? (busy)
   a London   b **Atlanta**   c Singapore

4 What's the _____ capital city in the world? (high)
   a **La Paz, Bolivia**
   b Kathmandu, Nepal
   c Lima, Peru

5 Which city has the _____ public transportation in the world? (expensive)
   a Seoul   b Mexico City   c **London**

c Answer **A**'s questions.

Which city has the best quality of life in the world—Tokyo, Copenhagen, or Miami?

10B WHAT ARE YOU GOING TO DO?
Student B

a Answer **A**'s questions.

b Ask **A** the questions below.

Tonight	• What / have for dinner tonight? • What / do after dinner?
Tomorrow	• / go to work (or school) tomorrow? • What / do in the evening?
Next weekend	• / go out on Friday night? What / do? • What / do on Sunday?

6 DESCRIBING YOUR HOME

a Read the website and the description of an apartment in Hermosa Beach, California. Would you like to stay there?

b Number the information in the order it comes in the description.

- [ ] Details about some of the rooms
- [ ] How far it is from Los Angeles
- [ ] What floor the apartment is on
- [ ] What rooms there are
- [ ] What services there are nearby
- [ ] What you can see from the apartment
- [ ] Where it is

c Look at the information about *so*.

> **so**
> *There's a sofa bed in the study, so you can use it as an extra bedroom.*
> We can use *so* to express a result or consequence, e.g.,
> *I was very tired, so I went to bed early.*
> *My office is near my house, so I walk to work.*

d You are going to write a description of your house or apartment for the website. First, make notes on the topics in **b**.

e Now write your description. Choose which of your ideas you want to use. Don't forget to say where you would like to go.

f Check your description for mistakes. Show it to other students. Whose house or apartment would you like to stay in?

◀ *p.63*

house swap

Home | How it works | Search | News and views | Join our community | Help

Do you want a cheap vacation? Write a description of your house or apartment, and say where <u>you</u> want to go. Post the description on our website, and find someone to swap homes with.

My home
Apartment near the beach

My apartment is on a quiet street in Hermosa Beach, California. It's on the second floor. It has two bedrooms, two bathrooms, a living room, a study, and a kitchen. The kitchen is small, but it has a stove, a refrigerator, and a dishwasher. There's a sofa bed in the study, so you can use it as an extra bedroom. The bedrooms have a great view of the beach and the Pacific Ocean. The apartment doesn't have a yard, but it has a community swimming pool. It's a 5-minute walk from stores, restaurants, and a bus stop. It's also about a 30-minute car ride from downtown Los Angeles.

Where I want to go
New York City, Buenos Aires, Phuket

7 A FORMAL EMAIL

a Read the advertisement and Marco's email. Complete the email with the words in the list.

> about   confirm   Dear   double   from
> hope   Sincerely   reservation   would

b Look at the information box and then write a similar email to the Bay House Bed and Breakfast.

- Decide how many nights you want to stay and the kind of room you need.
- Ask an *Is there | Are there…?* question.

🔍 **Formal emails (e.g., to a hotel or Bed and Breakfast, a language school, etc.)**

Beginning
Dear Mr. / Mrs. / Ms. + last name, or
Dear Sir / Madam if you don't know the person's name
Use a comma (,) NOT a colon (:)
Dear Mr. Brown, NOT ~~*Dear Mr. Brown:*~~

Middle
Don't use contractions.
I would like to make a reservation.
NOT ~~*I'd like to…*~~

End
Use a comma (,)
Sincerely,
Your first name + last name

◀ *p.79*

The Bay House
Bed and Breakfast in Bath, Maine

Gary and Rebecca Brewster and their family welcome you to their 100-year-old home in a small town in Maine.

5 double bedrooms, 3 single, and a family suite   ☐ TV   📶 WiFi

The Bay House – reservation
From: Marco Perez [marco84@gomail.com]
To: thebayhouse@bedbreakfastonline.net

¹_____ Mr. and Mrs. Brewster,

I ²_____ like to make a ³_____ for a ⁴_____ room and a single room for two nights, ⁵_____ June 24th to June 26th.

We ⁶_____ to arrive by car at ⁷_____ 5:00 in the afternoon on the 24th. Is there a place where we can park near your house?

Could you please ⁸_____ the reservation?

⁹_____,

Marco Perez

Listening

(3 49))

1   He was an English writer.
    He was born in the 16th century.
    He was married with three children.
    He was born in Stratford-upon-Avon.
    He is famous for his plays, for example,
    Hamlet and *Macbeth*.
2   She was born in London in 1932 to
    American parents.
    She was a famous actress.
    She was dark-haired and very beautiful.
    She was best friends with Michael Jackson.
    She was famous for her dark blue eyes.

(3 52))

… and finally on the news today the story of
two soccer fans who missed the big match.
   Last week, Chelsea played Arsenal at
Chelsea's famous stadium, Stamford Bridge in
west London. It was the match that soccer fans
all over the world wanted to watch. Charles
Spencer's daughter and a friend were among
the lucky people with tickets. The girls were
in Althorp, which is about 85 miles from
London, and they decided to go by taxi. But
when the taxi stopped in a small village, it was
clear that something was wrong. They were in
Stamford Bridge, but not at the Chelsea
stadium. The driver had typed Stamford
Bridge into his GPS. But unfortunately,
Stamford Bridge is also a small village in the
north of England – and that's where they were!
Of course, they missed the match.

(3 60))

Interviewer When was your memorable
   night?
David Te puedo decir exactamente, fue el
   once de julio del dos mil diez. I can tell you
   exactly, it was July 11th, 2010.
Interviewer Why do you remember the
   date?
David Because it was the final of the World
   Cup, Spain against Holland.
Interviewer Where were you?
David Well, I'm a flight attendant and that
   day I was in Acapulco in Mexico.
Interviewer Who were you with?
David I was with three other Spanish flight
   attendants.
Interviewer Where did you go to watch the
   match?
David We didn't go out. We watched the
   match in the hotel restaurant.
Interviewer And what did you wear to watch
   the match?
David We wore Spanish soccer shirts that we
   bought in a store, and we also had red and
   yellow scarves.
Interviewer Tell me about the night. What
   did you do?

David Well, the match was on in the
   afternoon Mexican time. We went down to
   the hotel restaurant early to get a good seat.
   There was a big screen. The restaurant was
   full of Spanish tourists. There was a great
   atmosphere.
Interviewer And Spain won the match, of
   course.
David Yes. It wasn't a good match, but when
   Spain got their winning goal everybody
   shouted and jumped up. It was amazing!
   When the match finished we all went
   out. We wanted to celebrate. We went to
   another restaurant near the beach, and it
   was full of Spanish people. Everyone was
   really happy. We had a great party!
Interviewer What was the weather like? Do
   you remember?
David Yes, it was a warm night. About 20
   degrees Celcius, I think.
Interviewer What time did you get back to
   your hotel?
David I can't remember exactly but very late,
   about three in the morning. Luckily, I had a
   free day the next day, so I didn't need to get
   up early.
Interviewer Why was this night so
   memorable?
David First, of course, because Spain won
   their first World Cup, but also because of
   the circumstances – we were very far away
   from Spain, thousands of kilometers away
   in another country, but we all felt very
   Spanish that night!

(3 64))

Rob So, Jenny, we have a free morning. What
   do you want to do?
Jenny Well, you're the expert on London life!
   What do you suggest?
Rob Well, we can go cycling.
Jenny I don't have a bike.
Rob We can rent bikes. It's easy.
Jenny That's cool.
Rob OK, great. So we can cycle through the
   parks, and you can see a bit of London. Oh,
   hang on. Uh, oh. It's Daniel. Daniel, hi!
Daniel Hi, Rob. You need to do an interview
   this morning, with an artist. He's at the
   Tate Modern.
Rob Can I do the interview on Monday?
Daniel Sorry, he can only do this morning.
Rob OK, send me the details.
Daniel Thank you very much, Rob.
Rob I'm sorry.
Jenny That's OK, I understand. Work is work!
Rob But I can meet you later, outside the Tate
   Modern. It's on the South Bank.
Jenny I can find it. I have a map, I can cycle
   there.
Rob Let's meet at twelve o'clock then.
Jenny Great.

(3 68))

Rob Sorry about the weather.
Jenny Yeah… but what a view! It's a great
   bridge too.
Rob It's the Millennium Bridge. It's not for
   cars, only for people. It was the first new
   bridge over the Thames in 100 years.
Jenny You sound like a tour guide!
Rob Sorry… I interviewed the architect last
   year. So what would you like to visit?
Jenny What is there to see?
Rob Well, we could see the Tate Modern first
   as we're here, and then we could go to the
   Globe Theatre. Do you like Shakespeare?
Jenny Not really. I studied too much
   Shakespeare in college. It's Daniel. Sorry.
   Hi, Daniel.
Daniel Hi, Jennifer. How's your free day?
   Are you enjoying London?
Jenny Absolutely. It's fantastic.
Daniel Listen, I have some free time today.
   Would you like to meet for lunch?
Jenny That's really nice of you, Daniel, but
   I'm sorry, I can't. I'm really far away from
   the office right now.
Daniel That's OK. No problem. Maybe
   another time?
Jenny Definitely. Bye.
Rob What did he want? Anything
   important?
Jenny Not at all. Hey, let's go inside the Tate
   Modern now.
Rob Yes, of course. There's a great restaurant
   on the top floor. The view is fantastic. The
   Tate Modern was a power station until
   1981. Did you know that?
Jenny I didn't. Do you know anything else
   about the Tate Modern?
Rob Thank you for asking. I know a lot about
   it actually.
Jenny Oh, great!

(4 6))

Then the detective questioned Barbara Travers.
Detective What did you do after dinner
   yesterday evening?
Barbara After dinner? I played cards with
   Gordon, and then I went to bed.
Detective What time was that?
Barbara It was about eleven thirty. I
   remember I looked at my watch.
Detective Did you hear anything in your
   father's room?
Barbara No. I didn't hear anything.
Detective Miss Travers, did you have any
   problems with your father?
Barbara No, I didn't have any problems
   with him at all. My father was a wonderful
   man and a wonderful father. I'm sorry,
   Detective.
Detective Don't worry, Miss Travers. No
   more questions.

4 7))

Next, the detective questioned Gordon Smith.

Detective What did you do after dinner, Gordon?

Gordon I played cards with Barbara. Then she went to bed.

Detective Did you go to bed then?

Gordon No. I stayed in the living room and I had a cup of tea. Then I went to bed.

Detective What time was that?

Gordon I don't remember exactly. I didn't look at the time.

Detective Did you hear anything during the night?

Gordon No, I didn't. I was very tired. I slept very well.

Detective You and Mr. Travers were business partners, weren't you?

Gordon Yes, that's right.

Detective And it's a very good business I understand.

Gordon Yes, Detective, it is.

Detective And now, it is your business.

Gordon Listen, Detective, I did not kill Jeremy. He was my partner and he was my friend.

4 8))

Finally, the detective questioned Claudia Simeone.

Detective What did you do yesterday evening, after dinner?

Claudia I went to my room and I took a bath and I went to bed.

Detective What time was that?

Claudia About 11 o'clock.

Detective Did you hear anything?

Claudia Yes. I heard somebody go into Jeremy's room. It was about 12 o'clock.

Detective Who was it?

Claudia It was Amanda, his wife.

Detective Are you sure? Did you see her?

Claudia Well, no, I didn't see her. But I'm sure it was Amanda.

Detective You were Mr. Travers's assistant, Claudia.

Claudia Yes, I was.

Detective Were you just his assistant?

Claudia What do you mean?

Detective Were you in love with Mr. Travers?

Claudia No, I wasn't.

Detective The truth please, Claudia.

Claudia Fine, Detective. Yes, I was in love with him, and he said he was in love with me. He said he wanted to leave his wife – Amanda – and marry me. I was stupid. I believed him. He used me, Detective! I was very angry with him.

Detective Did you kill him?

Claudia No, Detective, I loved Jeremy.

4 9))

Before dinner, Gordon met with Jeremy in the library.

Gordon Happy birthday, Jeremy.

Jeremy Ah, thanks, Gordon.

Gordon Listen, Jeremy, I want to talk to you about Barbara.

Jeremy Barbara? What's the problem?

Gordon It's not exactly a problem. I am in love with her, and I want to marry her.

Jeremy Marry Barbara? Marry my daughter! Are you crazy? Never! You don't love Barbara. You only want her money!

Gordon That's not true, Jeremy. I love her.

Jeremy Listen to me. If you marry Barbara, when I die all my money goes to Claudia.

Gordon To Claudia? To your assistant?

Jeremy Yes.

Gordon Is that your last word, Jeremy?

Jeremy Yes, it is.

Amanda Dinner everybody!

Reader At midnight, Gordon was in the living room. He finished his tea and went upstairs.

Jeremy Who is it? Gordon?

4 14))

Barbara Let's go upstairs. Follow me. Be careful. The ceiling is very low here.

Leo It's a very old house.

Barbara Yes, the house is three hundred years old. My family lived here for nearly eighty years. There are six bedrooms. This was my father's bedroom.

Kim Is there heat in the house?

Barbara Yes, there is. Why do you ask? Are you cold?

Kim Yes, it's very cold in here.

Leo That's because we're from California.

Barbara Let's go and see the other bedrooms.

Leo Yes, of course.

Leo Well, what do you think, Kim? I love it! Don't you?

Kim I'm not sure. There's something about the house I don't like.

Leo Kim, it's perfect for the kids. Think of the yard. And it's a real authentic country house. What do you say?

Kim I suppose so. If you're sure.

Leo I am sure! Mrs…uh, Barbara. We want it. We want to rent the house.

Barbara Excellent.

Leo When can we move in?

Barbara As soon as you like.

4 15))

Leo Hello.

Waiter Good evening, sir, madam. What can I get you?

Kim How about a coffee? I'm still cold.

Waiter Yes, madam. And you, sir?

Leo You know, I'm cold, too. I'll also have a coffee, thanks.

Waiter Here you are!

Leo Well, here's to our new house!

Kim Yes!

Waiter You're new around here, aren't you?

Leo Yes, that's right.

Kim We just rented the big house on Darwin Road.

Waiter Which house? The Travers family's house?

Leo Yes.

Waiter Oh.

Leo Is something wrong?

Waiter Who showed you the house?

Kim Barbara. The old lady who lived there before.

Waiter Ahh, Barbara. Old Mr. Travers's daughter. Some people thought that she was the one who did it. She never married, of course.

Kim The one who did what? What happened? Why didn't she marry?

Waiter Didn't she tell you?

Leo Tell us what?

Waiter About the murder.

Leo & Kim Murder??

Waiter Yes, Mr. Travers was murdered in that house in 1958… in his bed.

Kim Oh, how horrible!

Waiter The man who killed Mr. Travers was Barbara's lover. The family never lived there again. They tried to sell the house, but nobody wanted to buy it. Not after a murder. That's why that house is always rented.

Leo Kim.

Kim Yes.

Leo Are you thinking what I'm thinking?

Kim Yes – I don't want to sleep in a house where somebody was murdered. Come on. Let's go to a hotel.

Waiter Hey, your coffee! You didn't drink your coffee! Ah, well.

4 24))

I arrived at Gosforth Hall late in the evening. I don't believe in ghosts, but yes, I felt a little nervous. I checked in, and the front-desk clerk gave me the key and showed me to my room.

I left my things in the room and came downstairs. There weren't many other guests in the hotel. There were only three. I sat in the lounge and I talked to the manager, Sara Daniels, about her hotel. Then I had a drink and at 12 o'clock, I went upstairs to my room.

Room 11 was on the top floor. I opened the door and turned on the light.

It was a very big room, very old, and yes, it was a little spooky. There was an old TV on a table – but there wasn't a remote control. I turned on the TV.

There was a movie on. I was happy to see that it wasn't a horror movie. I decided to watch the movie, but I was tired after my long trip and after half an hour, I went to sleep.

4 25))

Stephen In the middle of the night, I suddenly woke up! I looked at my watch. It was two o'clock in the morning. The TV was off! But how? There was no remote control, and I didn't get up and turn it off. The light was on, but suddenly the light went off, too. Now I was scared! I couldn't see anything strange, but I could feel that there was somebody or something in the room. I got out of bed and turned on the light and TV again. Little by little I started to relax, and I went to sleep again. When I woke up, it was morning. I had breakfast and checked out. I left the hotel about ten o'clock.

Interviewer So the question is, did you see the ghost?

Stephen No, I didn't see the ghost, but I definitely felt something or somebody in the room when I woke up in the night.

Interviewer Were you frightened?

Stephen Yes, I was! Very frightened!

Interviewer Would you like to spend another night in the hotel?

Stephen Definitely, yes.

Interviewer Why?

Stephen Well, I'm sure there was something strange in that room. I can't explain the television and the light. I want to go back because I want to see the ghost.

4 32)))

Host Good afternoon and welcome to today's edition of *Get Ready! Cook!* And a big round of applause for today's contestants, Jack and Liz. Hello, Jack. So, do you like cooking?

Jack I love it. I cook dinner every evening at home.

Host How about you, Liz?

Liz Yes, I'm the cook in my family, too. I cook every day of course, but what I really like is cooking for friends on the weekend.

Host OK, so you know the rules. In the bag there are six ingredients, just six ingredients. You have an hour to make three dishes, an appetizer, a main course, and a dessert. Apart from the ingredients in the bag, you can also use basic ingredients like pasta, rice, eggs, sugar, salt, pepper, and so on. OK? Are you ready? Let's open the bag. And today's ingredients are a chicken, some carrots, some onions, three oranges, some cream cheese, and some dark chocolate. OK, Jack and Liz. You have five minutes to decide what to make, and then it's Get ready! Cook!

4 33)))

Host Liz and Jack, you have two more minutes, so I hope you're almost ready. OK. Time's up. Stop cooking now, please. OK, Jack. What did you make?

Jack For the appetizer, there's carrot and orange soup, for the main course I made chicken breasts filled with cream cheese, and for dessert I made pancakes with chocolate sauce.

Host That all looks delicious. And you, Liz?

Liz I made a carrot and onion salad with orange dressing. Then for the main course, I made pasta with creamy chicken sauce, and for dessert, chocolate and orange mousse.

Host It all looks good, too. But now, the moment of truth. Let's taste your dishes…

4 34)))

Host OK, Jack. Let's try your soup. Mmm, that's delicious. It's a great combination, carrot and orange. Is there any onion in the soup?

Jack Yes, one onion.

Host It's very good, but next time maybe you could add a little cream, not much, just a little. OK, now the chicken. Mmm, that's

nice. Not very original, but very tasty. And finally, the pancakes. They look beautiful… and they taste great. Now Liz, let's try your dishes. The salad first. Mmm, it's nice, but the taste of onion is very strong. How many onions did you use?

Liz Three.

Host I think maybe two are enough for this salad. OK, the pasta. Mmm, it's very good but it needs a little more salt and pepper. And finally, the mousse. That's a beautiful mousse, Liz.

Liz Thank you.

Host Mmm, and it tastes wonderful, absolutely delicious.
Well, congratulations to you both. I loved all your dishes – but only one of you can win – and today's winner is…Jack!

4 42)))

Host Question 1. What is the approximate population of Vietnam? Is it a 68 million, b 78 million, or c 88 million?

Contestant 1 I think it's c, 88 million.

Host c is the right answer! Question 2. How many calories are there in a Big Mac? Is it a 670, b 540, or c 305?

Contestant 2 I think it's a, 670.

Host Final answer?

Contestant 2 Final answer, 670.

Host I'm sorry, the right answer is b. A Big Mac has 540 calories. And Question 3. How far is it from New York City to Los Angeles? Is it a about 2,500 miles, b about 1,500 miles, or c about 3,100 miles?

Contestant 3 About 2,500 miles.

Host Are you sure?

Contestant 3 Yes. I'm sure.

Host a is the right answer!

4 45)))

Host Good evening. Welcome to *Quiz Night*. Tonight's show comes from New York City. And our first contestant is Colleen from Miami. Hi, Colleen. Are you nervous?

Colleen Yes, a little.

Host Well, just try to relax. The rules are the same as always. I'm going to read you some sentences, and you have ten seconds to say if the sentence is true or false. If you get the first answer right, you win 500 dollars. Then for each correct answer you double your money, so if you get the second answer right, you win 1,000 dollars, and for the third correct answer you win 2,000 dollars. For eight correct answers you win 64,000 dollars. But if you get an answer wrong, you lose all the money. Remember you can also call a friend, so if you're not sure about one of the answers, you can call your friend to help you. Is that OK, Colleen?

Colleen Yes, OK.

4 46)))

Host OK Colleen, first question for 500 dollars. The North Pole is colder than the South Pole. True or false?

Colleen The North Pole is colder than the South Pole. Uh, false.

Host Correct. The South Pole is much colder, because it's much higher than the North Pole. In the summer, the average temperature at the North Pole is 32 degrees Fahrenheit, but at the South Pole it's minus 15. Now, for 1,000 dollars, carrots are sweeter than tomatoes. True or false?

Colleen Uh, I think it's true.

Host Correct. It's true. Carrots are about five percent sugar, but tomatoes, even though they are a fruit and not a vegetable, don't have any sugar at all. OK, for 2,000 dollars, a proton is heavier than an electron.

Colleen I think it's true.

Host Correct. A proton is more than 1,800 times heavier than an electron. Next, for 4,000 dollars, The White House is bigger than Buckingham Palace. True or false?

Colleen The White House is bigger than Buckingham Palace. Uh, false.

Host Correct. Buckingham Palace has 775 rooms, but the White House has only 132 rooms. Next, for 8,000 dollars, oranges are healthier than strawberries. True or false?

Colleen Uh, true. No, uh, false.

Host Do you want to call a friend?

Colleen No, I think it's false.

Host Correct. An orange has 70 milligrams of vitamin C, but a cup of strawberries, a normal serving, has 98. OK, for 16,000 dollars, female mosquitoes are more dangerous than male mosquitoes.

Colleen Uh, true.

Host Correct. Female mosquitoes are the ones that bite. Male mosquitoes don't bite. OK, Colleen, for 32,000 dollars, in judo a green belt is better than a blue belt. True or false?

Colleen Uh, I'm sure that's false. My brother does judo. False.

Host Correct. The order of belts in the lower stages of judo is white for a beginner, then yellow, orange, green, blue, brown, and black. And finally, the last question. Be very careful, Colleen. If you get it right, you win 64,000 dollars, but if you get it wrong, you get nothing. Are you ready?

Colleen Yes, ready.

Host OK, for 64,000 dollars, hepatitis A is worse than hepatitis B. True or false?

Colleen Uh… uh…

Host Quickly, Colleen, your time is almost up.

Colleen I want to call a friend.

Host OK, Colleen. So, who do you want to call?

Colleen Kevin.

Host Is he your boyfriend?

Colleen Yes.

Host OK then. Hello, Kevin?

Kevin Yes.

Host I'm calling from *Quiz Night*. Colleen needs some help. You have 30 seconds, Kevin. Here she is.

Colleen Hi Kevin.

Kevin Hi Colleen.

Colleen Listen, Kevin. It's the last question. Hepatitis A is worse than hepatitis B. True or false?

Kevin Uh, I think it's true. Hepatitis A, yes, that's the serious one.

Colleen Are you sure?

Kevin Yes, definitely!

Host Time's up. OK Colleen, true or false?

Colleen True.

Host Final answer?

Colleen Final answer. True.

Host I'm sorry, Colleen, it's false. Hepatitis B is much more serious. You can die from it. You had 32,000 dollars, but now you go home with nothing.

Colleen Ooh, Kevin. You wait until I see him…

(4) 49))

Jenny Thanks for showing me around London yesterday. I had a great time.

Rob Me, too. So, what did you do last night?

Jenny Nothing really. I had a lot of work to do. Emails, phone calls… What did you do?

Rob I wrote my article about the artist that I interviewed yesterday morning.

Jenny Can I see it?

Rob Sure, it's on my laptop. Hang on a second. There.

Jenny Sorry. Hi, Eddie.

Eddie Happy birthday, Jenny!

Jenny Thanks! But listen, I can't talk right now.

Eddie Oh, sure.

Jenny I'm in the office.

Eddie I'll call you back.

Jenny Yeah, later.

Eddie OK.

Jenny OK. Sorry, but it's my birthday today.

Rob Really?! Happy birthday! Maybe we could have dinner tonight?

Daniel Jennifer.

Jenny Oh, hi Daniel.

Daniel I'd like to take you out for dinner this evening.

Jenny This evening?

Daniel Yes, for a working dinner. We have a lot to talk about before you go back to New York. I know a very good restaurant.

Jenny Oh, uh… yes, of course.

Daniel Great. See you later.

Jenny Yes, sure. Sorry, Rob.

(4) 55))

Daniel So, Jenny, I hear it's your birthday today.

Jenny Yes, that's right.

Daniel Well, Happy Birthday! How do you normally celebrate?

Jenny Oh, nothing special. Maybe I go out for dinner with friends or see a movie.

Daniel Well, we could go out somewhere, after dinner.

Waiter Would you like a dessert?

Jenny Not for me, thanks.

Daniel OK, no.

Waiter Coffee?

Jenny A decaf espresso.

Daniel The same for me, please.

Waiter Two decaffeinated espressos. Certainly, sir.

Daniel You know Jenny, you've got beautiful eyes.

Jenny I get them from my mother. Anyway,

what are your plans for the July edition of the magazine?

Daniel The, er, July edition? I um…

Jenny I have to take this. Sorry.

Daniel No problem.

Jenny Hi, Barbara.

Barbara Jenny, just a quick call. We really like your idea about Rob Walker. He's a great writer.

Jenny So can I ask him?

Barbara Yes. Go ahead.

Jenny That's great.

Barbara Good luck. I hope he says yes.

Jenny Me, too.

Daniel Good news?

Jenny Uh, yeah. That was Barbara my boss from the New York office. She just gave me a little birthday present.

Daniel So, would you like to go somewhere else?

Jenny I'm sorry, Daniel. I'm a little tired.

Daniel Yes, of course. Waiter, could I have the bill, please?

(5) 8))

Host On today's travel program, Alan Marks is going to tell us about CouchSurfing, a new way of traveling. Alan, what exactly is CouchSurfing?

Alan Well, CouchSurfing is an exciting and cheap way of traveling and seeing new places. It's a very simple idea. When you visit another city, you stay in somebody's apartment or house. That person, the host, gives you a room and a bed, and if he or she doesn't have a bed, then you can sleep on their couch, or sofa.

(5) 9))

Host Do you have to pay for the bed?

Alan No, you don't. It's completely free. CouchSurfers usually take a small present for the host or maybe they can help with the housework or make a meal. But you never pay any money.

Host How do you find these people?

Alan Well, there is a website called CouchSurfing.org. First, you go there and create a profile. Then you search for the city you want to visit, and you look for people there who are offering a bed. When you find somebody, you send them an email and then you can agree on the day or days that you want to stay. The website is free.

Host And do you have to offer a bed in your house?

Alan No, not if you don't want to. You can just be a guest or you can be a host and offer a room in your house, or you can do both things. It's up to you.

Host Is CouchSurfing safe?

Alan Yes, it is. You have a lot of information on the website about the person you are going to stay with. Every time a person stays with a host, they write a report, either positive or negative, and you can read all these reports. Also, you can email the person before you go and ask any questions you want.

Host Does the host usually show you his or her city?

Alan Well, it depends on the person. Some hosts take their guests to see some of the sights, but others don't. It depends when you visit, too. Some hosts take their guests out on the weekends, but are too busy during the week. But hosts usually recommend things to do, so you often see things that tourists don't usually see.

Host And can I CouchSurf all over the world?

Alan Of course. In fact, you can visit 230 countries and more than 70,000 cities.

(5) 15))

Part 2

"Well I have a problem with my boyfriend. We argue all the time. I'm not sure that he loves me. I want to know if we're going to stay together." "Please choose five cards, but don't look at them." Jane took five cards. The fortune-teller put them on the table face down. He turned over the first card. "Ah, this is a good card. This means you're going to be very lucky." "But am I going to stay with my boyfriend?" Jane asked. "Maybe," said the fortune-teller. "We need to look at the other cards first."

(5) 17))

Part 4

The fortune-teller turned over a card with two rings. "Now I can see everything clearly. You are going to leave your boyfriend and go away with the other man, with Jim…to another country. And very soon you're going to get married." "Married? To Jim? But am I going to be happy with him?" "You're going to be very happy together. I'm sure of it." Jane looked at her watch. "Oh, no, look at the time. I'm going to be late for work." She stood up, left a $50 bill on the table, and ran out of the room.

(5) 30))

One of the first things I noticed in Valencia is that people eat out a lot. They spend a lot of time in cafes. You find people having breakfast or tea, not just lunch and dinner. People who work go out to have coffee, they don't have it in their office. In restaurants, one thing that really surprised me was that when people go out in big groups, the men all sit at one end of the table and the women at the other.

Another thing I notice, maybe because I'm a woman myself, is what Spanish women are like, or Valencian women maybe. Of course, I'm a foreigner, but I find that the women here talk very fast and very loudly, much more than the men. Women dress very well, especially older women, and they always look immaculate!

Finally, there's a myth that the Spanish don't work hard, but I don't think it's true, it's just that they work different hours. People have a long lunch break, but they leave work very late.

Interviewer Today, most people spend a lot of time every day online, but do men and women use the Internet in the same way?

Expert Research shows that in general, they use the Internet in different ways. For example, men and women both use the Internet to send emails, but men send more work emails, while women send more personal emails to friends and family.

Interviewer What about online shopping?

Expert As you can imagine, women do more Internet shopping than men. They often use online stores to buy things for the house, clothes, toys, and so on. Men, on the other hand, prefer buying things on auction sites like eBay.

Interviewer What other sites are more popular with men?

Expert News sites are more popular with men than with women. Men also like visiting sports sites where they can find out, for example, game scores. In general, men use the Internet a lot for fun. They download music and play games much more than women do.

Interviewer What do women do more than men?

Expert Well, women often use the Internet to get information about health and medicine. And they are also more interested in websites that give them advice, for example, websites that give advice about how to be good parents, or diet websites that help them to lose weight. They also use the Internet for directions much more than men. They use websites like Google maps when they need to go somewhere new. And they use social networks like Facebook more than men do.

Interviewer Are there some things that both men and women do?

Expert Yes, they both use the Internet to book tickets for trains and planes, and to book hotels. They also both use online banking, for example, to pay bills or make transfers.

5 38)))

Jenny Rob!
Rob Jenny, hi. Sorry I'm a bit late.
Jenny No problem.
Rob Really?
Jenny Really!
Rob I got your message.
Jenny Would you like a coffee or something?
Rob No, I'm fine thanks. So what did you want to talk about? You think London is the best city in the world and you don't want to go home.
Jenny Not exactly. We'd like you to come to New York.
Rob Me? To New York?!
Jenny I talked to Barbara about you. You know, Barbara, my boss? She loves your articles, too. So, would you like to come over to New York and work for us? Just for a month. And write a column for *New York 24seven*. And maybe a daily blog?

Rob Wow, sounds great! What could I call it? *An Englishman in New York*?
Jenny Why not! Are you interested?
Rob Yes, very. It's amazing! But I need to think about it.
Jenny Of course.
Rob When do I need to decide?
Jenny Before the end of the week?
Rob OK, great. Thank you.
Jenny And now, I really have to go.

5 42)))

Jenny Where is it? Where's my phone?!
Rob Are you looking for this?
Jenny Rob! I can't believe it! My phone! You're a hero, thank you so much.
Rob No problem. It gave me a chance to see you again. And I had more time to think about your offer.
Jenny And?
Rob I'd love to accept. I really want to come and work in New York.
Jenny That's great, Rob! I'm so happy.
Rob Me, too. Oh, you had a call from Eddie. I didn't answer it. Is he going to meet you at the airport?
Jenny Eddie? No. He's at college in California.
Rob In California? Does he teach there?
Jenny Teach? No, he's a student.
Rob A student?
Jenny Well, he's only 19. Eddie's my brother.
Announcement Next departure flight 232 to New York is now ready for boarding.
Jenny I need to go.
Rob Well, have a good journey.
Jenny Thanks, Rob. Bye.
Rob Bye. And see you in New York!

5 49)))

1 Yes, I have. I don't usually see movies more than once or twice, but I've probably seen *It's a Wonderful Life*, the old Frank Capra movie, at least six or seven times because it's on TV every Christmas. It's usually on just after lunch on Christmas Day, which is when I'm full and a little sleepy, and I want to sit on the sofa and watch a movie. Actually, I think it's a great movie.

2 Yes, *The Empire Strikes Back*, the second *Star Wars* movie, well, the fifth episode in the series. I've seen it about twenty times probably. It's my favorite movie of all time, and when I meet a girl, I always watch it with her. It's a kind of test. If she doesn't like the movie, then I think that our relationship isn't going to work.

3 Yes, I have. *Flashdance*. I've seen it, oh, more than a hundred times. I absolutely love it. I love the music, and the movie just makes me feel good. Whenever I feel depressed I think, OK, I'm going to watch *Flashdance*. It always makes me feel better. I've bought the DVD three times because after you've played a DVD a lot, it doesn't work well.

5 51)))

Jess So, where are you going to take me for my birthday?
Matt I want to take you somewhere really nice. Have you been to *The Peking Duck* on 24th Street?
Jess On 24th Street. Yes, I have.
Matt Oh, no! When did you go there?
Jess Last month. I went with some people from work.
Matt OK. Somewhere else. Have you ever eaten at *Appetito* on 2nd Avenue? They make delicious pasta.
Jess I know. I've been there twice. But we could go there. I love Italian food.
Matt No, listen. Why don't we go back to *Luigi's*? We had an amazing meal last time. Do you remember? The Italian waiter sang for you. It was so romantic!
Jess No, I don't remember.
Matt You don't?
Jess No, I don't remember because it wasn't me. I've never been to *Luigi's*.
Matt Oh. My bad memory again.
Jess So, who did you go there with? With your ex-girlfriend?
Matt No, no, I went there with…my sister. Yes, with my sister.
Jess Your sister, huh? Let's forget it. I don't think I want to go out on my birthday.

7

7A simple past of *be*: *was / were*

President Reagan's wife **was** an actress. (3) 44))
She **wasn't** in class yesterday. **Was** she sick?
The Beatles **were** famous in the 1960s.
Where **were** you last night? You **weren't** at home.

+			−		
I / He / She / It	**was** there.		I / He / She / It	**wasn't** there.	
You / We / They	**were** there.		You / We / They	**weren't** there.	

?			✓	✗
Was	I / he / she / it	famous?	Yes, I **was**.	No, I **wasn't**.
Were	you / we / they		Yes, you **were**.	No, you **weren't**.

- We use *was / were* to talk about the past.
- We often use *was / were* with past time expressions, e.g., *yesterday, last night, in 1945*, etc.
- We use *was / were* with *born*: *I **was born** in Vietnam.*

7B simple past: regular verbs

I **played** tennis this morning. (3) 53))
We **watched** a good movie on TV last night.
My grandfather **lived** in São Paulo when he was young.
I **studied** Korean when I was at school.

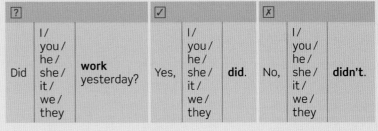

+		−	
I / You / He / She / It / We / They	**worked** yesterday.	I / You / He / She / It / We / They	**didn't work** yesterday.

?		✓		✗	
Did	I / you / he / she / it / we / they	**work** yesterday?	Yes,	I / you / he / she / it / we / they	**did**.	No,	I / you / he / she / it / we / they	**didn't**.

- We use the simple past for finished actions in the past.

spelling rules for regular verbs		
base form	**past**	**spelling**
watch play	watch**ed** play**ed**	add *-ed*
live	live**d**	add *-d*
stop	stop**ped**	one-syllable verbs: one vowel + one consonant = double consonant
study	stud**ied**	consonant + *y* > *ied*

- **Contraction:** *didn't = did not*.
- Regular verbs in the past + end in *-ed*, e.g., *worked, lived, played*.
- The simple past is the same for all persons (*I, you, she*, etc.).
- Use auxiliaries *did / didn't* + base form for simple past ? and −. *Did* is the past of *do*.

7C simple past: irregular verbs

I **went** to Canada last month. (3) 59))
I **didn't go** to Toronto.
Did you **go** to Montreal?

- Use the irregular past form only in + sentences: *I **saw** a movie last night.*
- Use the base form after *did / didn't*: *Did you see a movie last night?* **NOT** *Did you saw…?* *I **didn't go** out last night.* **NOT** *I didn't went…*
- Remember the word order in questions: auxiliary, subject, base form, e.g., *Did you go out last night?* or question word, auxiliary, subject, base form, e.g., *Where did you go?*
- There is a list of irregular verbs on page 165.

base form	past +	past −
go	went	didn't go
have	had	didn't have
get	got	didn't get
teach	taught	didn't teach
hear	heard	didn't hear
feel	felt	didn't feel
leave	left	didn't leave
lose	lost	didn't lose
meet	met	didn't meet
see	saw	didn't see
wear	wore	didn't wear
speak	spoke	didn't speak
do	did	didn't do

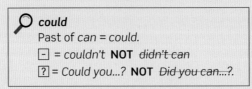

🔍 **could**
Past of *can* = *could*.
− = *couldn't* **NOT** *didn't can*
? = *Could you…?* **NOT** *Did you can…?*

7A

a Complete the simple past sentences with *was / wasn't* or *were / weren't*.

simple present	simple past
My father's a painter.	My grandfather _was_ a painter, too.
1 Today is Monday.	Yesterday _____ Sunday.
2 Where are you now?	Where _____ you yesterday?
3 I'm in Brazil.	I _____ in Peru last month.
4 Is it hot today?	_____ it hot yesterday?
5 The cafe isn't open now.	It _____ open this morning.
6 My neighbors aren't at home.	They _____ at home yesterday.
7 We're in Tokyo now.	We _____ in Kyoto yesterday.
8 They're tired.	They _____ tired last week.

b Complete the dialogues with *was, wasn't, were,* or *weren't*.

A _Were_ you and Miguel at the concert last night?
B Yes, we [1]_____.
A [2]_____ it good?
B No, it [3]_____. The singer [4]_____ terrible.
A [5]_____ the tickets expensive?
B Yes, they [6]_____.
A Where [7]_____ your mother born?
B She [8]_____ born in Argentina in 1955.
A [9]_____ her parents Argentinian?
B No, they [10]_____. Her father [11]_____ German and her mother [12]_____ from the US.

◄ *p.52*

7B

a Rewrite the sentences in the simple past with *yesterday*.

Present	**Past**
I watch TV.	_I watched TV yesterday._
1 We study English.	_____
2 Do you listen to the news?	_____
3 He doesn't cook dinner.	_____
4 Does she play sports?	_____
5 They work late.	_____
6 I use the Internet at work.	_____
7 She talks to her friends.	_____
8 My brother doesn't dance.	_____

b Complete the sentences with a verb in the simple past.

not call	cry	dance	finish	not listen	play

We _finished_ work late yesterday.

1 I _____ my mother on her birthday.
2 The movie was very sad. _____ you _____?
3 My brother _____ video games all day yesterday.
4 I _____ to the news this morning because I was late.
5 _____ Sarah _____ with Martin at the party?

◄ *p.54*

7C

a Complete the text with the verbs in parentheses in the simple past.

Last weekend, I _went_ (go) to New York City with some friends. We [1]_____ (meet) at the train station at 7:30 a.m. Our train [2]_____ (leave) at 7:45 a.m. In the morning, we [3]_____ (buy) some souvenirs. Then, we [4]_____ (have) lunch at a Chinese restaurant. In the evening, we [5]_____ (see) a play at Lincoln Center. We [6]_____ (get) home very late that night. We all [7]_____ (feel) very tired but very happy.

b Complete the questions in the simple past.

Did you go out last night? Yes, I did.

1 What _____? I wore jeans.
2 Where _____ your friends? We met in a cafe.
3 What time _____? We got home late.
4 How _____ home? We went home by taxi.
5 _____ a good time? Yes, we had a great time.

c Correct the information using the word in parentheses.

They got home at midnight. (11 p.m.)
They didn't get home at midnight. They got home at 11.

1 She wore a red dress. (blue)
_____

2 I left work early. (late)
_____

3 We went by train. (bus)
_____

4 He lost his cell phone. (wallet)
_____

5 You had a sandwich. (salad)
_____

◄ *p.57*

8

8A simple past: regular and irregular verbs

1 be **4 11** 》

- [+] I **was** born in Japan.
  They **were** late for class yesterday.
- [–] She **wasn't** at home last night.
  You **weren't** very nice to her.
- [?] **Were** you sick yesterday?
  When **was** he born?

2 regular verbs

- [+] I really **liked** the present.
  She **wanted** to be a doctor.
- [–] She **didn't enjoy** the concert.
  They **didn't arrive** until very late.
- [?] **Did** you **watch** the game last night?
  When **did** you **finish** the book?

3 irregular verbs

- [+] I **went** to Seoul last summer.
  She **slept** on the sofa.
- [–] He **didn't come** home last night.
  They **didn't hear** the music.
- [?] **Did** you **speak** to your sister yesterday?
  Where **did** you **have** lunch?

1 The past of *be* is *was/were*. We add *not* to make negatives and invert the subject and verb to make questions.

2 Regular verbs add *-ed* or *-d* in the simple past [+], e.g., *like–liked*, *want–wanted*.

3 Irregular verbs change their form in the simple past [+], e.g., *go–went*, *see–saw*.

- Regular and irregular verbs (except *can*) use:
  – *didn't* + base form to make negatives, e.g., *I didn't like it. She didn't see him.*
  – *did* + subject + base form to make questions, e.g., *Did you want to come? Where did she go?*

> 🔍 **can/could**
> The past of *can* is *could*. We add *not* to make negatives (*I couldn't find my glasses.*) and reverse the subject and verb to make questions (*Could you use your cell phone on the mountain?*).

8B *there is / there are, some / any* + plural nouns

	Singular		Plural	**4 16** 》
[+]	**There's** a garage.		**There are** some pictures on the wall.	
[–]	**There isn't** a swimming pool.		**There aren't** any plants in the room.	
[?]	**Is there** a bathroom downstairs?		**Are there** any neighbors with children?	
✓	Yes, **there is**.		Yes, **there are**.	
✗	No, **there isn't**.		No, **there aren't**.	

there is / there are

- We use *there is / there are* to say that somebody or something exists. We use *there is* + a singular noun and *there are* + plural nouns.
- *There is* is often contracted to *There's*. *There are* is not usually contracted.
- When we talk about a list of things, we use *there is* if the first word in the list is singular or *there are* if the first word in the list is plural:
  *In my bedroom, **there's a** bed, two chairs, and a desk.*
  *In the living room, **there are** two armchairs and a sofa.*

a / an, some and any

- We often use *there is / there are* with *a / an*, *some*, and *any*.
- Use *some* and *any* with plural nouns. *Some* = not an exact number.
- Use *some* in [+] sentences and *any* in [–] and [?].

> 🔍 **There is or It is?**
> Be careful. *There is* and *It is* are different.
> **There's** a key on the table. **It's** the key to the kitchen.

8C *there was / there were*

	Singular		Plural	**4 27** 》
[+]	**There was** an old TV.		**There were** only three guests.	
[–]	**There wasn't** a remote control.		**There weren't** any more people.	
[?]	**Was there** a ghost?		**Were there** any windows?	
✓	Yes, **there was**.		Yes, **there were**.	
✗	No, **there wasn't**.		No, **there weren't**.	

- *there was / were* is the past of *there is / are*.

8A

a Complete the dialogue using the simple past of the verbs in parentheses.

A Where <u>were</u> (be) you last night at 8:00?
B I ¹_____ (be) at home, Detective. With my wife. We ²_____ (be) at home all evening.
A What ³_____ you _____ (do)?
B We ⁴_____ (watch) TV and then we ⁵_____ (have) a light dinner. We ⁶_____ (not be) hungry. After that, we ⁷_____ (go) to bed.
A What time ⁸_____ you _____ (go) to bed?
B About 10 o'clock.
A ⁹_____ you _____ (hear) a noise during the night?
B No, I ¹⁰_____ (not hear) anything.

b Complete the text with the simple past of the verbs in parentheses.

Last night, I <u>was</u> (be) asleep in my room when a strange noise ¹_____ (wake) me up. I ²_____ (not want) to leave my room because I ³_____ (feel) very scared. Then I ⁴_____ (hear) the noise again, so I ⁵_____ (decide) to go and investigate. When I ⁶_____ (turn on) the light in the kitchen, a bird ⁷_____ (fly) out of the window. I ⁸_____ (close) the window so that the bird ⁹_____ (not can) come in again, and then I ¹⁰_____ (go) back to bed.

◀ p.61

8B

a Complete with ⊞ or ? of *There's* or *There are*.

<u>There's</u> a dishwasher in the kitchen.
<u>Are there</u> any people in the room?
1 _____ any books on the shelf?
2 _____ a toilet downstairs?
3 _____ some stairs over there.
4 _____ a rug on the floor.
5 _____ some pictures on the wall.
6 _____ a shower in the bathroom?
7 _____ some chairs in the yard.
8 _____ a lamp in the bedroom?
9 _____ a bicycle in the garage.
10 _____ any glasses in the cupboard?

b Write ⊞, ⊟, or ? sentences with *there is/are + a/an, some* or *any*.

⊞ trees/the yard   *There are some trees in the yard.*
1 ⊞ table/the kitchen _____.
2 ? fireplace/the living room _____?
3 ⊟ plants/your apartment _____.
4 ? people/the hall _____?
5 ⊞ pictures/your bedroom _____.
6 ⊟ TV/the kitchen _____.
7 ⊞ computer/the study _____.
8 ⊟ chairs/the dining room _____.
9 ? mirror/the bathroom _____?
10 ⊟ car/the garage _____.

◀ p.63

8C

a Complete the dialogue with the correct form of *there was* or *there were*.

A How many guests <u>were there</u> in the hotel?
B ¹_____ four including me. ²_____ a Brazilian tourist and ³_____ two businessmen.
A ⁴_____ a restaurant?
B No, ⁵_____, but ⁶_____ a coffee shop.
A ⁷_____ a refrigerator in your room?
B Yes, ⁸_____, but ⁹_____ any drinks in it.
A How many beds ¹⁰_____?
B One. A double bed.

b Complete the sentences with *there was/were/ wasn't/weren't + a/an*, or *some/any*.

There were some ghosts in the haunted hotel I stayed in.
1 My sister didn't take a shower because _____ spider in the bathtub.
2 We couldn't watch the news because _____ TV in our room.
3 I couldn't sleep on the plane because _____ noisy children behind me.
4 They couldn't play tennis because _____ tennis balls.
5 She didn't have a coffee because _____ cups.
6 He took a photo because _____ beautiful view.
7 They couldn't park near the restaurant because _____ parking lot.
8 I couldn't work in the hotel because _____ computer.

◀ p.65

9

9A countable / uncountable nouns

an apple   *three apples*   *rice*   *meat*

- There are two kinds of nouns in English, countable (C) and uncountable (U).

  C = things you can count, e.g., *apples*. C nouns can be singular (*an apple*) or plural (*apples*).

  U = things you can't count.

  butter, meat **NOT** ~~*two butters, three meats*~~

  U nouns are usually singular.

- Some nouns can be C or U, but the meaning is different.

an ice cream (C)   *some ice cream* (U)

a / an, some / any

	countable	uncountable 4 30)))
⊞ We need	**an** apple. **some** apples.	**some** butter.
⊟ We don't need	**a** tomato. **any** tomatoes.	**any** rice.
❓ Do we need	**an** orange? **any** oranges?	**any** sugar?

- We use *a / an* with singular C nouns; *a / an* = one.
- We use *some* ⊞ with plural C nouns and with U nouns; *some* = not an exact number or quantity.
- We use *any* in ⊟ and ❓ with plural C nouns and with U nouns.

> 🔍 **some in ❓**
>
> We use *some* in ❓ to ask for and offer things.
> *Can I have **some** apples, please?*
> *Would you like **some** coffee?*

9B quantifiers: *how much / how many, a lot of*, etc.

uncountable (singular)	short answers	full answers 4 37)))
How much sugar do you eat?	A lot. A little. Not much. None.	I eat **a lot of** sugar. I eat **a little** sugar. I don't eat **much** sugar. I don't eat **any** sugar.

countable (plural)		
How many cookies do you eat?	A lot. A few. Not many. None.	I eat **a lot of** cookies. I eat **a few** cookies. I don't eat **many** cookies. I don't eat **any** cookies.

- We use *How much…?* with uncountable (U) nouns and *How many…?* with plural countable (C) nouns.
- We use:

  a lot (of) with C and U nouns for a **big quantity**.

  a little / not…much with U nouns for a **small quantity**.

  a few / not…many with C plural nouns for a **small quantity**.

  not…any (*none* in short answers) for **zero quantity**.

a lot of and *much / many*

- In ⊞ sentences we usually use *a lot of*.
- In ⊟ sentences and ❓, we usually use *much* and *many*: *I don't drink **much** water. Do you drink **much** coffee?*
- It is also possible to use *a lot of* in ⊟ and ❓: *Do you drink **a lot of** coffee? I don't eat **a lot of** vegetables.*

9C comparative adjectives

*Is your sister **older than** you?*   4 47)))
*Buckingham Palace is **bigger than** the White House.*
*Female mosquitoes are **more dangerous than** males.*
*My new job is **better than** my old one.*
*The traffic is always **worse** in the evening.*

- Use comparative adjectives + *than* to compare two things, people, etc.

adjective	comparative	spelling
old cheap	old**er** cheap**er**	one-syllable adjectives: add *-er*
big hot	big**ger** hot**ter**	adjectives ending one vowel + one consonant: double consonant, add *-er*
dry healthy	dr**ier** health**ier**	one- or two-syllable adjectives ending consonant + *y* > *-ier*
famous expensive	**more** famous **more** expensive	two- or more syllable adjectives: *more* + adjective
good bad far	**better** **worse** **farther / further**	irregular

9A

a Write *a*, *an*, or *some* + a
food / drink word.

some bread

1 _____   5 _____
2 _____   6 _____
3 _____   7 _____
4 _____   8 _____

b Complete the dialogue with *a*, *an*, *some*, or *any*.

A What can we make for your brother and his girlfriend?
B Let's make <u>a</u> lasagna.
A Good idea. Are there ¹____ onions?
B Yes. And there are ²____ tomatoes, too.
A Great!
B Oh, no! There isn't ³____ pasta!
A Oh. Wait a minute. I bought ⁴____ chicken yesterday. Are there ⁵____ potatoes?
B Yes, there are.
A Good. So we can have chicken and mashed potatoes. Do we have ⁶____ fruit?
B Yes. I think we have ⁷____ oranges. Why?
A You can make ⁸____ fruit salad for dessert. There's ⁹____ apple and ¹⁰____ bananas, too.
B OK. Let's start cooking.

◀ *p.69*

9B

a Complete with *How much | How many*.

<u>How much</u> sugar do you put in your tea?

1 _____ butter do you use?
2 _____ cans of soda did she drink?
3 _____ oil do I need?
4 _____ chocolates were in that box?
5 _____ rice do you want?
6 _____ coffee does he drink?
7 _____ bottles of water did you buy?
8 _____ cans of tuna do we have?
9 _____ orange juice is there in that carton?
10 _____ cookies did you eat?

b (Circle) the correct word or phrase.

I don't put (much)/ *many* salt on my food.
1 We don't eat *a lot of | a lot* candy.
2 **A** How much chocolate do you eat? **B** *A little | A few.*
3 My friends don't drink *much | many* coffee.
4 **A** How much fruit do you buy? **B** *A lot | A lot of.*
5 We eat *a lot of | much* fish. We love it!
6 **A** Do your children drink any milk? **B** No. *Not much | Not many.*
7 Donna ate her hamburger, but she didn't eat *much | many* French fries.
8 **A** How many vegetables do you eat? **B** *Any | None.* I don't like them.
9 I have a cup of tea and *a few | a little* cereal for breakfast.
10 **A** Do you eat *much | many* meat?
  B No, I don't eat *no | any* meat. I'm a vegetarian.

◀ *p.70*

9C

a Write the comparative form of
these adjectives.

big   *bigger*
1 high   _____
2 dirty   _____
3 dangerous _____
4 good   _____
5 thin   _____
6 slow   _____
7 healthy   _____
8 far   _____
9 comfortable _____
10 bad   _____

b Complete with a comparative adjective + *than*.

My sister is <u>younger than</u> me. She's only 18. (young)

1 The farmer's market is _____ the supermarket for vegetables. (cheap)
2 Italian is _____ for Spanish students _____ it is for English students. (easy)
3 It rains a lot in the spring. April is _____ July. (wet)
4 This restaurant is _____ when it first opened. (busy)
5 Come in the summer. The weather is _____ in the spring. (good)
6 I love science. I find it _____ history. (interesting)
7 Cuzco is _____ from the ocean _____ Lima. (far)
8 I'm _____ my brother. He's very tall. (short)
9 The situation is _____ it was last year. (bad)
10 Skiing is _____ I thought it was. (difficult)

◀ *p.73*

10

10A superlative adjectives

It's **the hottest** month of the year. ⑤ 5))
It's **the most dangerous** road in the world.
She's **the best** student in the class.
Monday is **the worst** day of the week.

- Use *the* + superlative adjective to say which is the (*biggest*, etc.) in a group.
- After superlatives, we use *in* (not *of*) + places, e.g., *the world*, *the class*.

adjective	comparative	superlative	spelling
cold high	col**der** high**er**	**the** cold**est** **the** high**est**	add -*est*
big hot	big**ger** hot**ter**	**the** big**gest** **the** hot**test**	double consonant, add -*est*
dry sunny	dr**ier** sunn**ier**	**the** dr**iest** **the** sunn**iest**	> -*iest*
dangerous	**more** dangerous	**the most** dangerous	*the most* + adjective
good bad far	**better** **worse** **farther/further**	**the best** **the worst** **the farthest/** **furthest**	irregular

10B *be going to* (plans)

I'm going to take a vacation next month. ⑤ 11))
I'm not going to study English.
Are you **going to take** a vacation, too?

	full form	contraction		
+	I **am** You **are** He / She / It **is** We **are** They **are**	I**'m** You**'re** He / She / It**'s** We**'re** They**'re**	**going to**	**take** a vacation next month. **study** English tonight.
-	I **am not** You **are not** He / She / It **is not** We **are not** They **are not**	I**'m not** You **aren't** He / She / It **isn't** We **aren't** They **aren't**	**going to**	**take** a vacation next month. **study** English tonight.

?			
Am I **Are** you **Is** he / she / it **Are** we **Are** they	**going to**	**take** a vacation next month. **study** English tonight.	

✓			✗	
Yes,	I **am**. you **are**. he / she / it **is**. we **are**. they **are**.	No,	I**'m not**. you **aren't**. he / she / it **isn't**. we **aren't**. they **aren't**.	

- We use *be going to* + verb (base form) to talk about future plans.
- We often use future time expressions with *going to*:
  tomorrow, next week, next year, etc.

10C *be going to* (predictions)

- We can use *be going to* + verb (base form) to make predictions (= to say what you think or can see is going to happen in the future).

I think it**'s going to** rain. ⑤ 19))
You**'re going to be** very happy.
I'm sure they**'re going to win**.

10A

a Write the opposite.

the smallest	*the biggest*
1 the coldest	_____
2 the most expensive	_____
3 the best	_____
4 the most difficult	_____
5 the driest	_____
6 the shortest	_____
7 the nearest	_____
8 the cleanest	_____

b Complete the sentences with a superlative. Use the adjectives in parentheses.

The tigers are *the most dangerous* animals in the zoo. (dangerous)

1 Our house is _____ house on the street. (big)
2 For me, Saturday is _____ day of the week. (good)
3 My bedroom is _____ room in our house. (small)
4 July is _____ month in my country. (hot)
5 My neighbors upstairs are _____ people in the world. (noisy)
6 _____ driver in my family is my dad. (bad)
7 Sophie is _____ student in our English class. (young)
8 _____ building in my town is the museum. (beautiful)

◀ p.76

10B

a Complete the sentences with the correct form of *be going to* and the verb in parentheses.

She doesn't have a car. *She's going to travel by train.* (travel)

1 We need a vacation. We _____ a hotel near the beach. (book)
2 Tomorrow is Saturday. I _____ in bed. (stay)
3 My sister wants to be a doctor. She _____ medicine. (study)
4 Laura and David are in love. They _____ married. (get)
5 Ian is busy. He _____ late tonight. (work)
6 Their house isn't very neat. They _____ housework this afternoon. (do)
7 It's raining. We _____ an umbrella. (take)
8 I have a problem at work. I _____ to my boss. (speak)

b Complete the sentences with *be going to* + a verb.

---
not buy   call   not come   eat
go   not see   sleep   watch

I'm staying with a friend. I*'m going to sleep* on the couch.

1 I need to talk to my mom. I _____ her tonight.
2 There isn't any food. What _____ we _____?
3 My friend is sick. She _____ to the party.
4 They don't have any money. They _____ any new clothes.
5 The Yankees are playing the Red Sox. _____ you _____ the game?
6 Our friends are away. We _____ them this week.
7 The children are tired. They _____ to bed.

◀ p.78

10C

a Write predictions for the pictures.

A	be catch make ~~play~~ send
B	the bus an email a nice day an omelet ~~tennis~~

He's going to play tennis.

1 _____.
2 _____.
3 _____.
4 _____.

b Complete the predictions with *be going to* and a verb.

---
be   break   not finish   forget   have
not like   not pass   tell   win

I'm a fortune-teller. *I'm going to tell* you about your future.

1 You're driving very fast! I'm sure we _____ an accident!
2 She's a very bad student. She _____ the exam.
3 Be careful with that glass! You _____ it!
4 We have a lot of homework. I'm sure we _____ it.
5 They're playing well. I think they _____ the game.
6 Look at the time. We _____ late.
7 Oh, no, it's a horror movie. I'm sure I _____ it.
8 He didn't put her number in his phone. He _____ it.

◀ p.81

11

11A adverbs (manner and modifiers)

adverbs of manner

They drive **dangerously**. 🔊 25))
He dresses **fashionably**.
She eats very **quickly**.
I work **hard**.
We speak English **well**.

- We use adverbs of manner to say <u>how</u> people do things.
- Adverbs usually go after the verb.
  *I speak English **very well**.*
  NOT ~~I speak very well English.~~

adjective	adverb	spelling
slow quick bad careful	slow**ly** quick**ly** bad**ly** careful**ly**	+ -ly
happy easy	happ**ily** eas**ily**	consonant + y > -ily
possible	possi**bly**	le > -ly
good fast hard	**well** **fast** **hard**	irregular

- Remember the difference between adjectives and adverbs:
  *I'm a **careful** driver. (careful is an adjective. It describes the noun, driver.)*
  *I drive **carefully**. (carefully is an adverb. It describes the verb, drive.)*

modifying adverbs: *very, really,* etc.

It isn't **very** expensive. 26))
She drives **incredibly** fast.
They speak **really** slowly.

- We use modifying adverbs with adjectives or other adverbs.
- They always go <u>before</u> the adjective or adverb.

> 🔍 **words ending in -ly**
> Not all words that end in -ly are adverbs, e.g., *friendly* = adjective.
> *He's a **friendly** person.*

11B verbs + infinitive: *want to, need to,* etc.

I **want to find** a new job. 🔊 31))
You **need to practice** every day.
When did you **learn to play** the guitar?
Would you like to be famous?

- Many verbs are followed by the infinitive.
- These include: *want, need, learn, promise, decide, plan,* and *hope*.

would like to

- *I would like to* = *I want to* (now or in the future).
- **Contractions**: 'd = would; wouldn't = would not.
- Use the infinitive after *would like*. *I **would like to learn**.*
  NOT ~~I would like learn.~~
- Remember you can also use *Would you like…?* to offer:
  ***Would you like** a drink?*
- *would like* is the same for all persons.

> 🔍 **would like and like**
> ***I'd like** to dance.* = I want to dance.
> ***I like** dancing.* = I enjoy it; I like it in general.

11C articles

1 *a / an*

A What's this? **B** It's **a** photo of my daughter. 37))
A What do they do? **B** Jim's **a** doctor. Sally's **an** engineer.
A How often do they have classes? **B** Three times **a** week.

2 *the*

Can you close **the window**, please?
Can you check their address on **the Internet**?
It's **the best** restaurant I know.

3 *a* or *the*?

Let's have **a** pizza. **The** pizzas are very good here.

4 no article

Men are usually more interested in sports than **women**.
She's **my mother's cousin**. That's **Tom's chair**!
Jim goes to **school** by **bus**.

1 We use *a / an*
  - to say what something is or what job people do.
  - in expressions of frequency.
2 We use *the*
  - when the speaker and hearer know the thing we are talking about: *Close **the window**.* = the one that is open.
  - when there is only one of something: *the Internet, the sun,* etc.
  - before superlative adjectives: *the biggest, the best,* etc.
3 We often use *a* the first time we mention a person or thing and then *the* the next time because it is now clear who or what we are talking about.
4 We don't usually use *the*
  - when we talk about people or things in general:
    ***Men** are more interested in sports than **women**.* (general)
    ***The women** in this class work harder than **the men**.* (specific)
  - before possessive 's. *She's my mother's cousin.* **NOT** ~~She's the my mother's cousin.~~
  - with the following:
    meals: *breakfast, lunch, dinner,* etc.
    places: *work, school, college, bed, home,* etc.
    by + transportation: *go by car, travel by train,* etc.

11A

a Adjective or adverb? (Circle) the correct form.

People drive really *dangerous* | *dangerously*.

1 He wrote down the phone number *careful* | *carefully*.
2 My neighbor's children aren't very *polite* | *politely*.
3 My niece plays the piano *beautiful* | *beautifully*.
4 Fast food is incredibly *unhealthy* | *unhealthily*.
5 Old people often walk very *slow* | *slowly*.
6 I bought a *real* | *really* cheap bag at the sale.
7 My friend sings very *good* | *well*.
8 My sister speaks Spanish *perfect* | *perfectly*.
9 We wear *casual* | *casually* clothes to work.
10 The view from the top is *incredible* | *incredibly* beautiful.

b Complete with adverbs from these adjectives.

bad	careful	easy	fast	good
hard	fashionable	perfect	quiet	

The buses and trains in Malmö run *perfectly* when it snows.

1 Can you talk _____, please? I'm trying to sleep.
2 Don't drive _____ when it's raining.
3 I don't like the ocean because I can't swim very _____.
4 She picked up the baby _____ and put him in the bathtub.
5 We're working _____ because we have an exam.
6 I always dress _____ when I go to a party.
7 We played _____ in the semifinal game and we lost 5–1.
8 She was the best athlete so she won the race _____.

◀ p.85

11B

a Complete the sentences with the infinitive form of a verb from the list.

be	buy	call	climb	drive	get married
go	leave	pass	see	stay	

Sam loves Africa. He wants *to climb* Mount Kilimanjaro.

1 I learned _____ a car when I was 17. I passed my test the first time!
2 Our refrigerator is broken. We need _____ a new one.
3 I wouldn't like _____ famous. I'm happy the way I am now.
4 He promised _____ his girlfriend after work.
5 The weather was terrible. We decided _____ at home.
6 My friend would like _____ Radiohead live. She loves them.
7 They're planning _____. Their wedding is on July 12th.
8 I studied hard last week. I hope _____ the exam.
9 Do you like animals? Would you like _____ on a safari?
10 She's enjoying the party. She doesn't want _____.

b (Circle) the correct form.

I hate *fly* | *flying* so I usually travel by train.

1 Would you like *have* | *to have* dinner with me tonight?
2 My grandmother learned *to drive* | *driving* when she was 62.
3 I'd like *to travel* | *traveling* around Asia.
4 I like *relax* | *relaxing* on weekends.
5 Do you want *to play* | *playing* soccer?
6 He's hoping *to have* | *having* more time when he retires.
7 Most people hate *to go* | *going* to the dentist.
8 I love *to read* | *reading* detective stories.
9 It's cold. You need *wear* | *to wear* a coat.
10 My mom doesn't like *to cook* | *cooking*.

◀ p.86

11C

a (Circle) the correct word or phrase.

How much time do you spend on *Internet* | *the Internet*?

1 My brother is *at college* | *at the college* studying math.
2 I'd like *cup of tea* | *a cup of tea*, please.
3 We're going to visit my aunt *on weekend* | *on the weekend*.
4 We have English classes *twice a week* | *twice week*.
5 I love reading *novels* | *the novels*.
6 Yolanda is *best* | *the best* student in our class.
7 My mom's *lawyer* | *a lawyer*.
8 He's *the man* | *a man* that I told you about yesterday.
9 Can you open *a door* | *the door* for me, please?
10 He had *breakfast* | *the breakfast* late this morning.

b Complete with *the*, *a* | *an*, or –.

I'm going to buy *a* new laptop next week.

1 What time do you finish ____ work?
2 We usually go to the movies once ____ month.
3 ____ children behaved very badly yesterday.
4 Lorena doesn't like ____ dogs.
5 I want to be ____ engineer when I finish studying.
6 ____ sun came out so we went for a walk.
7 Can you pass ____ salt, please?
8 My mom chose ____ most expensive dessert.
9 Last year, we went on vacation by ____ train.
10 This is Joanne. She's ____ very good friend.

◀ p.89

12

12A present perfect

1 **A Have you seen** his new movie? (5 45))
  B Yes, **I've seen** all his movies.
  She hasn't read any Harry Potter books.
2 **Have you ever read** a Russian novel?
  Sarah's never worked in a big company.
3 **Have you finished** the exercise?
  Your parents **have arrived**. They're in the living room.

1 We use the present perfect when we talk or ask about things that have happened in the past, but when we don't say when.
2 We often use the present perfect with *ever* (= at any time in your life) and *never* (= at no time in your life).
3 We also use the present perfect to talk about something that has recently happened.

	full form of *have*	contraction	past participle of main verb
+	I have You have He / She / It has We have They have	I've You've He / She / It's We've They've	seen that movie.
−	I have not You have not He / She / It has not We have not They have not	I haven't You haven't He / She / It hasn't We haven't They haven't	

?		
Have **Has**	I / you / we / they he / she / it	**seen** that movie?

✓		
Yes,	I / you / we / they he / she / it	**have.** **has.**

✗		
No,	I / you / we / they he / she / it	**haven't.** **hasn't.**

- To make the present perfect use *have / has* + the past participle of the verb.
- *'s* = *has* in present perfect.
- Past participles of regular verbs are the same as the simple past.

base form	simple past	past participle
like	liked	liked
want	wanted	wanted

- Past participles of irregular verbs are sometimes the same as the simple past, e.g., *read*, but sometimes different, e.g., *seen*.

base form	simple past	past participle
read /rid/	read /rɛd/	read /rɛd/
see	saw	seen

(There is a list of irregular past participles on p.165)

12B present perfect or simple past?

A Have you been to Luigi's? **B** Yes, **I have**. (5 52))
A When **did you go** there? **B** I **went** last weekend.
A Who **did you go** with? **B** I **went** with some people from work.
I've been to New York twice. **I went** to visit my sister – she's married to an American.

- We often use the **present perfect** to ask about or tell somebody about a past action for the first time. We don't ask / say when the action happened: *Have you been to Luigi's?* *I've been to New York twice.*
- We then use the **simple past** to ask / talk about specific past details: *When did you go there? I went to visit my sister.*
- We use the simple past **NOT** the present perfect with *when* and past time expressions, e.g., *yesterday, last week*:
  When did you see it? **NOT** *When have you seen it?*
  I saw it last week. **NOT** *I've seen it last week.*

been or **gone**?

I've **been** to Brazil. (5 53))
My sister's **gone** to Brazil to study Portuguese.

- *Been to* and *gone to* have different meanings. *Been* is the past participle of *be*, and *gone* is the past participle of *go*.
- In the present perfect, we use *been to* (**NOT** *gone to* or *been in*) to say that somebody has visited a place.
  I've been to the US three times. Have you been to the new Vietnamese restaurant on George Street?
- We use *gone to* when somebody goes to a place and is still there:
  My parents have gone to the US for their vacation. They don't come back until Saturday.
- Compare: *Nick has been to Paris* = He visited Paris and came back at some time in the past.
  Nick has gone to Paris, = He went to Paris, and he is in Paris now.

12A

a Write the sentences with contractions.

I have seen the movie. *I've seen the movie.*

1 She has not read the book.
2 You have not washed the dishes.
3 We have done the housework.
4 He has been sick.
5 They have not eaten Japanese food before.

b Write ⊞, ⊟, and ⍰ sentences in the present perfect.

⊞ I / meet a famous actor.
I've met a famous actor.

1 ⊞ I / forget your name
2 ⊟ my boyfriend / wear his new shirt
3 ⍰ you / speak to your boss
4 ⊟ they / do their homework
5 ⍰ your brother / work in New York
6 ⊞ the train / leave the train station
7 ⊟ we / take any photos
8 ⍰ the children / eat all the cookies
9 ⊟ my girlfriend / call me today
10 ⊞ Janet / leave her book at home

c Write a sentence in the present perfect for each picture. Use the verbs in the box.

| break buy fall go read win |

They've won the cup.

1 _____ his leg.
2 _____ to the beach.
3 _____ off his motorcycle.
4 _____ the newspaper.
5 _____ a new car.

◀ p.92

12B

a Circle the correct form.

Have you ever eaten / Did you ever eat at Appetito?

1 I *haven't bought / didn't buy* any new clothes recently.
2 My boyfriend *has given / gave* me a ring for my last birthday.
3 They *'ve spent / spent* a lot of money yesterday.
4 *Have you ever won / Did you ever win* a competition?
5 My friends *have had / had* a party last weekend.

b Circle the correct form.

Let's go to the Peking Duck. I've never *been / gone* there.

1 The secretary isn't here. She's *gone / been* to the bank.
2 I've never *gone / been* to the US.
3 My neighbors aren't at home. They've *gone / been* on vacation.
4 Have you ever *gone / been* abroad?
5 We have lots of food. We've *gone / been* to the supermarket.

c Put the verbs in parentheses in the present perfect or simple past.

A *Have you ever traveled* abroad? (travel)
B Yes, I *went* to Peru last year. (go)
A ¹_____ you ever _____ any countries in Asia? (visit)
B Yes, I have. I ²_____ to South Korea a few years ago. (go)
A Who ³_____ you _____ with? (go)
B My husband. It was a work trip and his company ⁴_____ for everything. (pay)
A How wonderful! How ⁵_____ you _____ there? (get)
B We ⁶_____. (fly)
A Where ⁷_____ you _____? (stay)
B We ⁸_____ a suite in a five-star hotel. It was beautiful! (have)
A ⁹_____ the company _____ you on any other trips recently? (take)
B No. My husband ¹⁰_____ working there a year later, so that was our only trip. (stop)
A Too bad!

◀ p.94

Days and numbers

4 HIGH NUMBERS

a Write the missing words or numbers.

_105_	a / one hundred and five
_____	two hundred
350	three hundred and _____
875	eight hundred _____ seventy-five
1,000	a / one thousand /ˈθaʊznd/
_____	one thousand five hundred
2,012	two thousand and _____
5,420	five thousand four _____ and twenty
_____	twenty-five thousand
100,000	a / one hundred _____
1,000,000	a / one million /ˈmɪlyən/
2,300,000	two million _____ hundred thousand

b Listen and check.

◀ p.72

go, have, get

a Match the verbs and pictures.

- ☐ by bus / by car / by plane /bʌs/ /kɑr/ /pleɪn/
- ☐ *1* for a walk /wɔk/
- ☐ home (*from school*) /hoʊm/
- ☐ out (*on Friday night*) /aʊt/
- ☐ <u>sho</u>pping /ˈʃɑpɪŋ/
- ☐ to a <u>res</u>taurant /ˈrɛstərənt/
- ☐ to bed (*late*) /bɛd/
- ☐ to church / to mosque / to temple /tʃɜrtʃ/ /mɑsk/ /ˈtɛmpl/
- ☐ to the beach /bitʃ/
- ☐ back (*to work*) /bæk/
- ☐ on va<u>ca</u>tion /veɪˈkeɪʃn/

- ☐ a car / a bike /kɑr/ /baɪk/
- ☐ long hair /lɔŋ ˈhɛr/
- ☐ <u>break</u>fast / lunch / <u>din</u>ner /ˈbrɛkfəst/ /lʌntʃ/ /ˈdɪnər/
- ☐ a drink /drɪŋk/
- ☐ a good time /gʊd taɪm/
- ☐ a <u>sand</u>wich /ˈsændwɪtʃ/
- ☐ a <u>sis</u>ter / a <u>bro</u>ther /ˈsɪstər/ /ˈbrʌðər/

- ☐ a <u>news</u>paper (= buy) /ˈnuzpeɪpər/
- ☐ a <u>ta</u>xi / a bus / a train (= take) /ˈtæksi/ /bʌs/ /treɪn/
- ☐ an <u>e</u>mail / a <u>le</u>tter (= receive) /ˈimeɪl/ /ˈlɛtər/
- ☐ dressed /drɛst/
- ☐ home (= arrive) /hoʊm/
- ☐ to the <u>air</u>port (= arrive) /ˈɛrpɔrt/
- ☐ up (*early*) /ʌp/

b (3 61))) Listen and check.

c Cover the expressions and look at the pictures. Test yourself or a partner.

d Take turns saying three things you did yesterday and three you did last week with *went*, *had*, or *got*.

> *Yesterday, I got up early. I had breakfast in a cafe. I went shopping...*

◀ p.57

go

have

get

The house

1 ROOMS

Match the words and pictures 1–9.

- ☐ a <u>bath</u>room /ˈbæθrum/
- ☐ a <u>bed</u>room /ˈbɛdrum/
- ☐ a <u>din</u>ing room /ˈdaɪnɪŋ rum/
- ☐ a ga<u>rage</u> /ɡəˈrɑdʒ/
- ☐ a hall /hɔl/
- ☐ a <u>kit</u>chen /ˈkɪtʃən/
- ☐ a <u>liv</u>ing room /ˈlɪvɪŋ rum/
- 1 a <u>stud</u>y / an <u>off</u>ice /ˈstʌdi/ /ˈɔfəs/
- ☐ a yard /yɑrd/

2 PARTS OF A ROOM

Match the words and pictures 10–14.

- ☐ a <u>bal</u>cony /ˈbælkəni/
- ☐ the <u>ceil</u>ing /ˈsilɪŋ/
- ☐ the floor /flɔr/
- ☐ the stairs /stɛrz/
- ☐ the wall /wɔl/

3 THINGS IN A ROOM

a Match the words and pictures 15–31.

- ☐ an <u>arm</u>chair /ˈɑrmtʃɛr/
- ☐ a <u>bath</u>tub /ˈbæθtʌb/
- ☐ a bed /bɛd/
- ☐ a <u>cup</u>board /ˈkʌbərd/
- ☐ a <u>fire</u>place /ˈfaɪərpleɪs/
- ☐ a lamp /læmp/
- ☐ a light /laɪt/
- ☐ a <u>mir</u>ror /ˈmɪrər/
- ☐ a plant /plænt/
- ☐ a re<u>frig</u>erator / a fridge /rɪˈfrɪdʒəreɪtər/ /frɪdʒ/
- ☐ a rug /rʌɡ/
- ☐ a shelf (shelves) /ʃɛlf/
- ☐ a <u>show</u>er /ˈʃaʊər/
- ☐ a <u>so</u>fa / a couch /ˈsoʊfə/ /kaʊtʃ/
- ☐ a stove /stoʊv/
- ☐ a <u>toi</u>let /ˈtɔɪlət/
- ☐ a <u>wash</u>ing ma<u>chine</u> /ˈwɑʃɪŋ məˈʃin/

> 🔍 **Heat and central air conditioning**
> Heat is a system that makes a house warm, usually using an oil, gas, or electric furnace. Central air conditioning is a system that makes a house cool.

b (4 12)) Listen and check **1–3**.

c Cover the words and look at the pictures. Test yourself or a partner.

◀ p.62

Prepositions: place and movement

1 PLACE

a Match the words and pictures.

- [ ] in /ɪn/
- [ ] in front of /ɪn frʌnt əv/
- [ ] on /ɑn/
- [ ] under /ˈʌndər/
- [1] behind /bɪˈhaɪnd/
- [ ] between /bɪˈtwin/
- [ ] across from /əˈkrɔs frəm/
- [ ] next to /nɛkst tu/
- [ ] over /ˈoʊvər/

b (4 21)) Listen and check.

c In pairs, ask and answer about the pictures.

Where's the ghost?

It's under the bed.

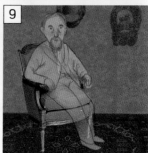

2 MOVEMENT

a Match the words and pictures.

- [ ] from…to /frəm/ /tu/
- [ ] into /ˈɪntu/
- [ ] out of /ˈaʊt əv/
- [ ] up /ʌp/
- [ ] down /daʊn/
- [1] toward /tɔrd/

b (4 22)) Listen and check.

c In pairs, ask and answer about the pictures.

Where's the ghost going?

It's going from the living room to room 11

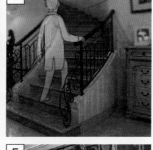

◄ p.65

Food

a Match the words and pictures.

Breakfast /'brɛkfəst/

☐ bread /brɛd/

☐ butter /'bʌtər/

☐ cereal /'sɪriəl/

☐ cheese /tʃiz/

☐ coffee /'kɑfi/

☐ eggs /ɛgz/

☐ jam /dʒæm/

☐ (orange) juice /dʒus/

☐ milk /mɪlk/

☐ sugar /'ʃʊgər/

☐ 1 tea /ti/

☐ toast /toʊst/

Lunch / dinner /lʌntʃ/ /'dɪnər/

☐ fish /fɪʃ/

☐ meat (steak, chicken, sausages) /mit/

☐ (olive) oil /ɔɪl/

☐ pasta /'pɑstə/

☐ rice /raɪs/

☐ salad /'sæləd/

Vegetables /'vɛdʒtəblz/

☐ carrots /'kærəts/

☐ French fries /frɛntʃ fraɪs/

☐ lettuce /'lɛtəs/

☐ mushrooms /'mʌʃrʊmz/

☐ onions /'ʌnyənz/

☐ peas /piz/

☐ potatoes /pə'teɪtoʊz/

☐ tomatoes /tə'meɪtoʊz/

Fruit /frut/

☐ apples /'æplz/

☐ bananas /bə'nænəz/

☐ oranges /'ɔrɪndʒɪz/

☐ a pineapple /'paɪnæpl/

☐ strawberries /'strɔbɛriz/

Desserts /dɪ'zərts/

☐ cake /keɪk/

☐ fruit salad /frut 'sæləd/

☐ ice cream /aɪs 'krim/

Snacks /snæks/

☐ candy /'kændi/

☐ chocolate /'tʃʊklət/

☐ cookies /'kʊkiz/

☐ potato chips /pə'teɪtoʊ tʃɪps/

☐ sandwiches /'sændwɪtʃɪz/

b **4 29**))) Listen and check.

c Cover the words and look at the pictures. Test yourself or a partner.

◀ *p.68*

Places and buildings

a Match the words and pictures.

- an <u>art</u> gallery /ˈɑrt gæləri/
- a bridge /brɪdʒ/
- a <u>bus</u> station /ˈbʌs steɪʃn/
- a <u>castle</u> /ˈkæsl/
- a church /tʃərtʃ/
- a de<u>part</u>ment store /dɪˈpɑrtmənt stɔr/
- a <u>hospital</u> /ˈhɑspɪtl/
- a <u>market</u> /ˈmɑrkət/
- a mosque /mɑsk/
- a mu<u>se</u>um /myuˈziəm/
- a <u>parking</u> lot /ˈpɑrkɪŋ lɑt/
- a <u>pharmacy</u> /ˈfɑrməsi/
- a po<u>lice</u> station /pəˈlis steɪʃn/
- a <u>post</u> office /ˈpoʊst ɑfəs/
- a <u>river</u> /ˈrɪvər/
- a road /roʊd/
- a <u>shopping</u> mall /ˈʃɑpɪŋ mɔl/
- a square /skwɛr/
- a street /strit/
- a <u>supermarket</u> /ˈsupərmɑrkət/
- a <u>temple</u> /ˈtɛmpl/
- a <u>theater</u> /ˈθɪətər/
- *1* a town <u>hall</u> /taʊn ˈhɔl/
- a train <u>station</u> /ˈtreɪn steɪʃn/

b (5 3)》 Listen and check.

c Cover the words and look at the pictures. Test yourself or a partner.

◀ *p.76*

Writing

Present	Simple past	Past participle
be /bi/	was /wəz/ were /wər/	been /bɪn/
become /bɪ'kʌm/	became /bɪ'keɪm/	become
begin /bɪ'gɪn/	began /bɪ'gæn/	begun /bɪ'gʌn/
break /breɪk/	broke /broʊk/	broken /'broʊkən/
bring /brɪŋ/	brought /brɔt/	brought
build /bɪld/	built /bɪlt/	built
buy /baɪ/	bought /bɔt/	bought
can /kæn/	could /kʊd/	—
catch /kætʃ/	caught /kɔt/	caught
come /kʌm/	came /keɪm/	come
cost /kɔst/	cost	cost
do /du/	did /dɪd/	done /dʌn/
drink /drɪŋk/	drank /dræŋk/	drunk /drʌŋk/
drive /draɪv/	drove /droʊv/	driven /'drɪvn/
eat /it/	ate /eɪt/	eaten /'itn/
fall /fɔl/	fell /fɛl/	fallen /'fɔlən/
feel /fil/	felt /fɛlt/	felt
find /faɪnd/	found /faʊnd/	found
fly /flaɪ/	flew /flu/	flown /floʊn/
forget /fər'gɛt/	forgot /fər'gɑt/	forgotten /fər'gɑtn/
get /gɛt/	got /gɑt/	got
give /gɪv/	gave /geɪv/	given /'gɪvn/
go /goʊ/	went /wɛnt/	gone /gɑn/
have /hæv/	had /hæd/	had
hear /hɪr/	heard /hərd/	heard
know /noʊ/	knew /nu/	known /noʊn/

Present	Simple past	Past participle
leave /liv/	left /lɛft/	left
lose /luz/	lost /lɔst/	lost
make /meɪk/	made /meɪd/	made
meet /mit/	met /mɛt/	met
pay /peɪ/	paid /peɪd/	paid
put /pʊt/	put	put
read /rid/	read /rɛd/	read /rɛd/
run /rʌn/	ran /ræn/	run
say /seɪ/	said /sɛd/	said
see /si/	saw /sɔ/	seen /sin/
send /sɛnd/	sent /sɛnt/	sent
sing /sɪŋ/	sang /sæŋ/	sung /sʌŋ/
sit /sɪt/	sat /sæt/	sat
sleep /slip/	slept /slɛpt/	slept
speak /spik/	spoke /spoʊk/	spoken /'spoʊkən/
spend /spɛnd/	spent /spɛnt/	spent
stand /stænd/	stood /stʊd/	stood
swim /swɪm/	swam /swæm/	swum /swʌm/
teach /titʃ/	taught /tɔt/	taught
take /teɪk/	took /tʊk/	taken /'teɪkən/
tell /tɛl/	told /toʊld/	told
think /θɪŋk/	thought /θɔt/	thought
understand /ʌndər'stænd/	understood /ʌndər'stʊd/	understood
wake /weɪk/	woke /woʊk/	woken /'woʊkən/
wear /wɛr/	wore /wɔr/	worn /wɔrn/
win /wɪn/	won /wʌn/	won
write /raɪt/	wrote /roʊt/	written /'rɪtn/

Vowel sounds

	usual spelling	! but also
tree	**ee** meet three **ea** speak eat **e** me we	people police key niece
fish	**i** his this win six big swim	English women busy
ear	**eer** cheer engineer **ere** here we're **ear** year hear	
cat	**a** thanks dance black Japan have stamp	
egg	**e** yes help ten pet red very	friend bread breakfast any said
chair	**air** airport stairs fair hair **are** square careful	their there wear
clock	**o** hot stop doctor job not box	father watch want
saw	**al** talk walk **aw** saw draw	water wrong bought
horse	**or** sport door short	four board
boot	**oo** school food **u**★ June use **ew** new flew	do fruit juice shoe

* especially before consonant + *e*

	usual spelling	! but also
bull	**u** full put **oo** good book look room	could would woman
tourist	A very unusual sound. euro Europe sure plural	
up	**u** bus lunch ugly run lucky cut	come brother son does young
computer	Many different spellings. /ə/ is always unstressed. um<u>bre</u>lla A<u>me</u>rica <u>fa</u>mous <u>se</u>cond a<u>go</u>	
bird	**er** her verb **ir** first third **ur** nurse turn	learn work world word
owl	**ou** out thousand house count **ow** how brown	
phone	**o**★ home close old don't **oa** road toast	slow low
car	**ar** are party start far	
train	**a**★ name make **ai** rain paint **ay** play day gray	break steak great eight they
boy	**oi** coin noise toilet **oy** toy enjoy	
bike	**i**★ nine twice **y** my why **igh** high night	buy

○ vowels   ⬭ vowels followed by /r/   ○ diphthongs

Consonant sounds

parrot

usual spelling		! but also
p	paper pilot Portuguese sleep	
pp	apple happy	

bag

b	be table job builder number	
bb	rubber	

key

c	credit card actor	architect
k	kitchen like	
ck	black back	

girl

g	green get angry big	
gg	eggs bigger	

flower

f	Friday fifteen wife	
ph	photo elephant	
ff	office coffee	

vase

v	very eleven live travel river love	of

tie

t	tea take student sit	liked dressed
tt	letter bottle	

dog

d	dance understand bad read	played tired
dd	address middle	

snake

s	sister stops	nice city
ss	stress actress	police

zebra

z	zero Brazil	
s	music please dogs watches	

shower

sh	shopping shoes Spanish fish	sugar sure
ti (+ **vowel**)	station information	

television

si (+**on**)	decision confusion	usually garage

thumb

usual spelling		! but also
th	think thirty throw bathroom fourth tenth	

mother

th	the these then other that with	

chess

ch	cheap children church	
tch	watch match	
t (+**ure**)	picture adventure	

jazz

j	January juice July enjoy	German manager
dge	bridge fridge	

leg

l	like little plane girl	
ll	small spelling	

right

r	red rich problem try	write wrong
rr	sorry terrible	

witch

w	window twenty Wednesday win	one once
wh	why when	

yacht

y	yellow yesterday young yes	
before **u**	use university music	

monkey

m	man Monday money swim	
mm	summer swimming	

nose

n	no never nine ran	know
nn	dinner thinner	

singer

ng	song England language thing long going	think bank

house

h	happy hungry hotel behind hall head	who whose

◯ voiced ◯ unvoiced

1B

American ENGLISH FILE

Workbook

Christina Latham-Koenig

Clive Oxenden

Paul Seligson

Paul Seligson and Clive Oxenden are the original co-authors of
English File 1 and *English File 2*

Contents

STUDY **LINK** iChecker SELF-ASSESSMENT CD-ROM

Powerful listening and interactive assessment CD-ROM

Your iChecker disc on the inside back cover of this Workbook includes:

- **AUDIO** – Download ALL of the audio files for the Listening and Pronunciation activities in this Workbook for on-the-go listening practice.

- **FILE TESTS** – Check your progress by taking a self-assessment test after you complete each File.

Audio: When you see this symbol iChecker, go to the iChecker disc in the back of this Workbook. Load the disc in your computer.

1

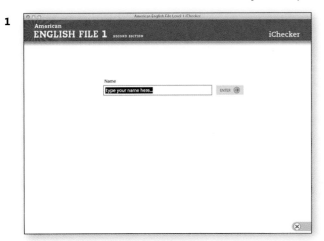

Type your name and press "ENTER."

2

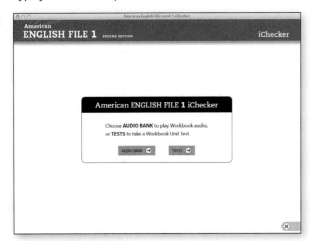

Choose "AUDIO BANK."

3

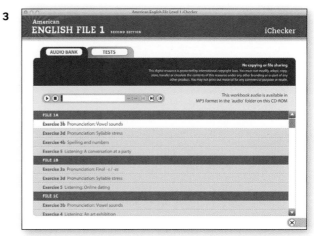

Click on the exercise for the File. Then use the media player to listen.

You can transfer the audio to a mobile device from the "audio" folder on the disc.

File test: At the end of every File, there is a test. To do the test, load the iChecker and select "Tests." Select the test for the File you have just finished.

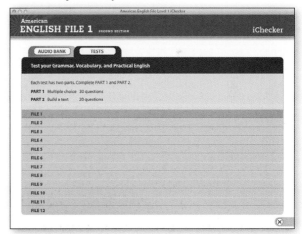

This page was intentionally left blank.

My life is a simple thing that would interest nobody.
It is a known fact that I was born, and that is all that is necessary.

Albert Einstein, German scientist

7A At the National Portrait Gallery

1 GRAMMAR simple past of *be*: *was / were*

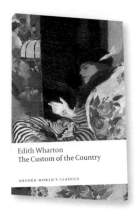

Edith Wharton
The House of Mirth

Edith Wharton
Ethan Frome

Edith Wharton
The Custom of the Country

a Complete the sentences with *was*, *were*, *wasn't*, or *weren't*.

A Who's that?
B It's Edith Wharton.
A Why ¹ <u>was</u> she famous?
B She ² _____ a writer.
A ³ _____ she Canadian?
B No, she ⁴ _____.
She ⁵ _____ American. She ⁶ _____ born in New York City in 1862.
A And ⁷ _____ she married?
B Yes, she ⁸ _____.

b Write questions and answers.

1 Alexander Graham Bell / sportsman? ✗
<u>Was Alexander Graham Bell a sportsman</u> ?
<u>No, he wasn't</u> .

2 Richard Burton and Elizabeth Taylor / actors? ✓
<u>Were Richard Burton and Elizabeth Taylor actors</u> ?
<u>Yes, they were</u> .

3 Jorge Luis Borges / writer? ✓
_____ ?
_____ .

4 The Beatles / from the US? ✗
_____ ?
_____ .

5 Robert Frost / politician? ✗
_____ ?
_____ .

6 I.M. Pei / composer? ✗
_____ ?
_____ .

7 Sofia Vergara / born / Columbia? ✓
_____ ?
_____ .

8 Frank Sinatra / singer? ✓
_____ ?
_____ .

9 J.R.R. Tolkien and C.S. Lewis / painters? ✗
_____ ?
_____ .

10 Michael Jackson / born / Britain? ✗
_____ ?
_____ .

c Complete the dialogues with present or past forms of *be*.

1 A What day <u>is</u> it today?
B Monday. Yesterday <u>was</u> Sunday.

2 A Hi. _____ your sister at home?
B No, she _____. She _____ here this morning, but now she _____ at work.

3 A I can't find my keys. Where _____ they?
B I don't know. They _____ on your desk this morning.

4 A Where _____ your new friend from?
B He _____ born in the US, but his parents _____ born in Singapore.

5 A Why _____ your boss angry yesterday?
B Because I _____ very late for work.

43

2 VOCABULARY word formation

a Make professions from these words. Use *a* or *an*.

1 invent   <u> *an inventor* </u>
2 write   <u>   </u>
3 dance   <u>   </u>
4 compose   <u>   </u>
5 music   <u>   </u>
6 paint   <u>   </u>
7 business   <u>   </u>
8 act   <u>   </u>
9 science   <u>   </u>
10 sail   <u>   </u>

b <u>Un</u>derline the stressed syllables, e.g. *an in<u>ven</u>tor*.

c Practice saying the words in **a**.

d Complete the sentences with *was / were* and a noun from **a**.

1 Francis Drake <u> *was a sailor* </u>.
2 Beethoven and Mozart <u> *were composers* </u>.
3 James Dean <u>   </u>.
4 Galileo <u>   </u>.
5 Freddie Mercury <u>   </u>.
6 The Wright brothers <u>   </u>.
7 F. Scott Fitzgerald <u>   </u>.
8 Howard Hughes <u>   </u>.
9 Degas and Toulouse-Lautrec <u>   </u>.

3 PRONUNCIATION sentence stress

iChecker Listen and repeat the conversation.

> **A** Who was Aaron Copland?
> **B** He was a composer.
> **A** Was he British?
> **B** No, he wasn't. He was American.
> **A** When was he born?
> **B** He was born in 1900.
> **A** Were his parents composers?
> **B** No, they weren't.

4 LISTENING

a **iChecker** Listen to a radio program about the greatest Americans of all time. Number the people in the order they come on the list.

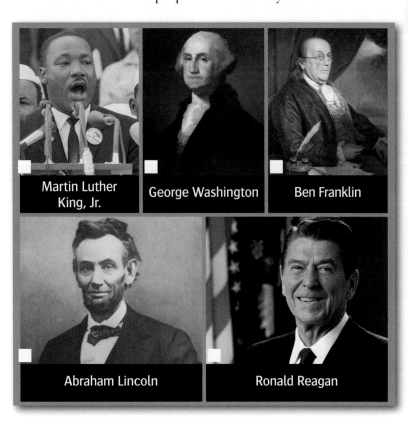

Martin Luther King, Jr.

George Washington

Ben Franklin

Abraham Lincoln

Ronald Reagan

b **iChecker** Listen again. Write T (true) or F (false).

1 Ben Franklin was a young newspaper owner.   *T*
2 George Washington was born on February 12, 1732.   ___
3 He was 76 when he died.   ___
4 Martin Luther King, Jr. was born on January 15th, 1929.   ___
5 He was young when he died.   ___
6 Abraham Lincoln was a painter.   ___
7 He was 56 when he died.   ___
8 The greatest American of all time was a singer.   ___

USEFUL WORDS AND PHRASES

Learn these words and phrases.

the (16th) century /ðə ˈsɛntʃəri/
killed /kɪld/
between (1816 and 1820) /bɪˈtwin/
be against (something) /bi əˈgɛnst/
be in love (with someone) /bi ɪn ˈlʌv/

7B Chelsea girls

1 GRAMMAR simple past: regular verbs

a Complete the sentences with a regular verb in the simple past, first in the affirmative and then in the negative.

| book download listen ~~miss~~ play study watch work |

1 Yesterday I ___*missed*___ my bus, but I ___*didn't miss*___ my train.
2 We _____ to the news, but we _____ to the weather.
3 My parents _____ French at school, but they _____ Spanish or Japanese.
4 My sister _____ the movie with me, but she _____ the soccer game.
5 The secretary _____ a table for lunch, but she _____ a taxi.
6 I _____ some music onto my laptop, but I _____ any movies.
7 The salesperson _____ last Saturday, but she _____ on Sunday.
8 My brother _____ tennis at school, but he _____ basketball.

b Order the words to make questions.

1 you / did / night / TV / What / on / last / watch?
   A ___*What did you watch on TV last night*___?
   B I watched the news.
2 did / game / the / time / end / What
   A _____?
   B At six o'clock.
3 your / presents / birthday / like / you / Did
   A _____?
   B Yes, I did. They were great!
4 did / college / your / in / brother / What / study
   A _____?
   B Modern Languages.
5 parents / your / arrive / late / Did
   A _____?
   B No, they didn't. They were early.
6 Brazil / your / in / friends / did / Where / live
   A _____?
   B Rio de Janeiro.
7 of / you / Did / at / the / cry / movie / end / the
   A _____?
   B Yes, I did. It was very sad.

8 time / work / did / What / arrive / Luisa / yesterday / at
   A _____?
   B At ten o'clock.

c Complete the questions and answers.

| 1990 1997 ~~1998~~ 2001 2004 2007 2009 |

When did it happen?

1 when / the Akashi-Kaikyo Bridge / open
   *When did the Akashi-Kaikyo Bridge open*_____?
   It opened in ___*1998*___.

2 when / Michael Jackson / die
   _____?
   He died in _____.

3 when / *Facebook* / start
   _____?
   It started in _____.

4 when / Princess Diana / die
   _____?
   She died in _____.

5 when / the first tourist / travel into space
   _____?
   It traveled into space in _____.

6 when / iPhones / first appear
   _____?
   They appeared in _____.

7 when / Tim Berners-Lee / create the World Wide Web
   _____?
   He created it in _____.

2 VOCABULARY past time expressions

Circle the correct answer.

1 I chatted with my friends for an hour **last night** / **yesterday night**.

2 My girlfriend finished college **ago two years** / **two years ago**.

3 They traveled abroad **last month** / **the last month**.

4 Did you call me **last morning** / **yesterday morning**?

5 It stopped raining **two hours ago** / **two ago hours**.

6 My brother worked in the city **last July** / **the last July**.

7 We watched that movie **before two weeks** / **two weeks ago**.

8 David booked the tickets **yesterday afternoon** / **last afternoon**.

9 Steve was born **in 1990** / **on 1990**.

10 I played golf **the day yesterday before** / **the day before yesterday**.

3 PRONUNCIATION -ed endings

a **iChecker** Listen to the words. Underline the word where -ed is pronounced /ɪd/.

1 booked	checked	wanted	walked
2 painted	arrived	finished	traveled
3 asked	waited	looked	stopped
4 called	played	chatted	listened
5 missed	watched	cooked	started
6 followed	decided	lived	relaxed

b **iChecker** Listen again and repeat the words.

4 READING

a Read the article and choose the best title.

1 The wrong match
2 The wrong destination
3 The wrong player

b Read the article again and answer the questions.

1 How old was Bojana when the incident happened?
2 Where was the tennis tournament?
3 How did she travel to Carlsbad?
4 Where did Bojana travel to first?
5 When did she arrive at the tournament?
6 Who did she play in her first match?
7 Did she win?

5 LISTENING

a **iChecker** Listen to four speakers describing bad trips. How did they travel (e.g., by car, etc.)?

1 _____ 3 _____
2 _____ 4 _____

b **iChecker** Listen again and match the speakers 1–4 to the sentences a–d.

Speaker 1 ☐
Speaker 2 ☐
Speaker 3 ☐
Speaker 4 ☐

A A stranger helped me.
B Someone in my family helped me.
C I started my trip twice.
D I didn't arrive at my destination.

USEFUL WORDS AND PHRASES

Learn these words and phrases.

GPS /dʒi pi 'ɛs/
surprised /sər'praɪzd/
arrive /ə'raɪv/
cry /kraɪ/
miss /mɪs/
text /tɛkst/
travel /'trævl/
country house /kʌntri 'haʊs/

Serbian tennis player Bojana Jovanovski was only 19 when she played in the San Diego Open. However, she almost missed the tournament. Her first match was in Carlsbad, California, so her agent booked a seat for her and gave her the ticket to Carlsbad. It was a long trip because Bojana needed to take three different planes. When she finally arrived in Carlsbad, she was surprised to find that the airport was empty. She waited for 15 minutes and then called Tournament Transportation. The problem was that Bojana was in Carlsbad, New Mexico and the transportation service was in Carlsbad, California where the tournament was. So, Bojana stayed in New Mexico for the night and then traveled to Carlsbad, California the next morning. She arrived only 30 minutes before the start of her match with the Italian player Roberta Vinci. Unfortunately, the day finished badly for Bojana because she lost the match 3-6, 6-4, 6-1. After that, she just wanted to go home!

Never be the first to arrive at a party or the last to go home, and never, ever be both.

Anonymous

7C A night to remember

1 GRAMMAR simple past: irregular verbs

a Change the sentences from the present to the past.

1 We meet in a café. (last night)
   We met in a café last night.

2 Mateo sees his friends after work. (last night)
   _____

3 Emily loses her keys. (yesterday)
   _____

4 We don't have dinner at home. (last night)
   _____

5 They leave work at 5:30. (yesterday)
   _____

6 Alex doesn't get up early. (yesterday morning)
   _____

7 My friend feels sick. (yesterday)
   _____

8 Junko doesn't go out during the week. (last week)
   _____

9 I don't wear glasses. (yesterday)
   _____

10 Luciana can't come to my party. (last year)
   _____

b Complete the questions in the dialogue.

A Where ¹ ___*did you go*___ last night?
B I went to that new sushi restaurant in town.
A ² _____ good?
B Yes, it was great.
A Who ³ _____ with?
B I went with my girlfriend.
A What ⁴ _____ ?
B I wore jeans and my new black shirt.
A What time ⁵ _____ home?
B We got home at about midnight.
A ⁶ _____ a taxi home?
B Yes. We didn't want to drive.
A Did ⁷ _____ a good time?
B Yes, we had a great time. The food was delicious!
A ⁸ _____ it expensive?
B Yes, it was.

2 VOCABULARY go, have, get

a ~~Cross out~~ the incorrect expression.

1 GO   to the beach   out   to a restaurant   ~~a bus~~
2 HAVE   lunch   a sandwich   for a walk   a sister
3 GET   dressed   a good time   up   an email
4 GO   to bed   a car   away   on vacation
5 HAVE   breakfast   a bike   short hair   18 years
6 GET   shopping   home   a newspaper   a taxi

b Complete the text with *went*, *had*, or *got*.

It was my wife's birthday last Saturday, so we ¹ ___*went*___ away for the weekend. I booked a hotel on the Internet, and on Friday we ² _____ the train to the coast. It was late when we arrived, so we just ³ _____ a sandwich and ⁴ _____ to bed. The next day, we ⁵ _____ up early and ⁶ _____ breakfast in the hotel. It was a beautiful day, so we ⁷ _____ to the beach. We took a swim in the morning, and in the afternoon we ⁸ _____ for a walk. In the evening, we ⁹ _____ dinner in an expensive French restaurant. The food was delicious! The next day was Sunday, so we ¹⁰ _____ back home again. The weekend was very short, but we ¹¹ _____ a great time.

3 PRONUNCIATION irregular verbs, sentence stress

a Look at the pairs of irregular verbs. Do they have the same vowel sound? Write **S** (the same) or **D** (different).

1 came   had   [D]
2 did   feel   [ ]
3 taught wore   [ ]
4 lost   spoke [ ]
5 met   went   [ ]
6 knew   saw   [ ]
7 heard   left   [ ]
8 took   could [ ]

b iChecker Listen and check. Then listen and repeat the irregular verbs.

c iChecker Listen and repeat the sentences. <u>Copy</u> the <u>rhythm</u>.

A **What** did you **do last night**?
B I **went** to the **movies**.
A **Who** did you **go** with?
B I **went** with a **friend**.
A **Where** did you **go** after the **movies**?
B We **went** to a **restaurant**.
  We **didn't have** an **expensive meal**.
  We **didn't get home late**.

4 LISTENING

a iChecker Listen to an interview about a memorable night. What did Melissa do?

b iChecker Listen again and answer the questions.

1 When was it?
_____.

2 Who was Melissa with?
_____.

3 Where were they?
_____.

4 When did she arrive in the city?
_____.

5 Where did they have a coffee?
_____.

6 Did they have a good time? Why (not)?
_____.

7 What did they have for dinner?
_____.

8 What time did they get home?
_____.

USEFUL WORDS AND PHRASES

Learn these words and phrases.

goal /goʊl/
moon /mun/
scarf /skɑrf/
screen /skrin/
embarrassed /ɪmˈbærəst/
memorable /ˈmɛmərəbl/
decide /dɪˈsaɪd/
take a swim /teɪk ə ˈswɪm/
know (somebody) a little /noʊ ə ˈlɪtl/

iChecker TESTS **FILE 7**

Practical English Getting lost

1 VOCABULARY directions

Complete the words.

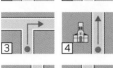

1 turn l_ef_t
2 go str_____ a_____
3 turn r_____
4 go p_____ the train station
5 on the c_____
6 across f_____
7 a b_____
8 at the tr_____ l_____

2 ASKING FOR DIRECTIONS

Complete the dialogue with these words.

exactly Excuse miss near say Sorry tell way Where's

A [1] _Excuse_ me, please. [2] _____ the train station?

B [3] _____, I don't live here.

A Excuse me. Is the train station [4] _____ here?

C The train station? It's near here, but I don't know [5] _____ where. Sorry.

A Excuse me. Can you [6] _____ me the [7] _____ to the train station, please?

D Yes, of course. Go past the hotel. Then turn left at the traffic lights. It's at the end of the street.

A Sorry, could you [8] _____ that again, please?

D Yes. Go past the hotel. Then turn left at the traffic lights and it's at the end of the street. You can't [9] _____ it!

A Thank you.

3 SOCIAL ENGLISH

Complete the sentences with the words in the box.

could course meet nice Maybe there ~~What~~ would

1 _What_ a view!
2 What _____ you like to visit?
3 What is _____ to see?
4 We _____ go to the art gallery.
5 Would you like to _____ for lunch?
6 That's really _____ of you.
7 _____ another time.
8 Yes, of _____.

4 READING

a Read the information about getting around in the US.

By bus

In the US, an economical way for traveling long distances is by bus. The most important company is Greyhound, which has frequent service between big cities. Greyhound is also a convenient way for traveling to smaller cities and towns that don't have other forms of transportation like trains or airplanes. Traveling by bus is usually cheap if you buy your ticket early and travel at times of the day that are not busy.

By car

Many people travel by car in the US. It can be expensive, and there is often a lot of traffic. However, traveling by car means that you can be independent and flexible. Also, a car with three or more passengers can be cheaper than public transportation. You can go quickly from one city to the next on freeways, but small roads are often more scenic and fun. Parking in big cities can be difficult and very expensive. Some cities like Denver, Baltimore, and Philadelphia have light rail train systems. You can park outside the city in a free parking lot and then take a light rail train downtown.

By train

Trains are generally faster and more comfortable than buses for long distance travel, but they can be a lot more expensive. There is only one train company that operates train service in the US, and that is Amtrak. Passengers can get information on timetables and fares from the Amtrak website, which also has a way to buy tickets. There are three types of tickets: coach class, business class, and first class. Tickets are cheaper if you buy them early.

b Read the information again. Write T (true) or F (false).

1 Taking a bus is a slow way to travel.   _T_
2 The best time to travel by bus is at quiet times.   ___
3 There isn't much traffic in the US.   ___
4 You need to pay for parking when you use
  light rail in Denver.   ___
5 You can buy tickets from Amtrak.   ___

c Match the highlighted adjectives to their meanings.

1 beautiful   _____
2 easy to do   _____
3 cheap   _____
4 easy to change something _____
5 happening often   _____

8A A murder story

1 GRAMMAR simple past: regular and irregular

a Read this police report. Complete the sentences with the simple past form of the verbs in parentheses.

POLICE REPORT

Bank robbery

We [1] *arrived* (arrive) at the bank at 9:36 in the evening, and we [2]_____ (park) our police car outside. The bank [3]_____ (be) closed and all the lights [4]_____ (be) off, but we [5]_____ (look) through the window. We [6]_____ (see) a person inside the bank. At first, we [7]_____ (not can) see who it was, but then he [8]_____ (open) the door and came out – it was Steven Potter. He [9]_____ (not run) away – he just walked slowly to his car, and then drove away. The next morning, we [10]_____ (go) to his house at 6:00 a.m. We [11]_____ (find) him in bed. He [12]_____ (not want) to speak to us, but we [13]_____ (take) him to the police station.

b Complete the questions with the correct form of the verbs in parentheses.

DETECTIVE   Where [1] *were you* at about 9:30 yesterday evening? (be)

STEVEN POTTER   I was at the movies. The movie [2] *started* at 9:00. (start)

D   What movie [3]_____? (see)

SP   I can't remember. It wasn't very good.

D   Hmm. Very interesting. And who [4]_____ to the movies with? (go)

SP   With my girlfriend.

D   [5]_____ the movie? (like)

SP   Yes, she thought it was very good.

D   What time [6]_____ the movie _____? (end)

SP   At about 10:30.

D   And what [7]_____ after you left the movies? (do)

SP   We went to a restaurant – La Dolce Vita on Main Street.

D   La Dolce Vita? I know it. Very good spaghetti. What time [8]_____ the restaurant? (leave)

SP   At about 12:00 a.m.

D   That's very late. [9]_____ home after that? (go)

SP   No, we went to a birthday party at Flanagan's. Then we went home.

D   How? [10]_____ a taxi? (get)

SP   No, we got a bus.

D   And what time [11]_____ to bed? (go)

SP   At about 4:00 a.m. Can I go home now? I'm tired.

D   No, I'd like to ask you some more questions...

2 VOCABULARY irregular verbs

a Complete the base form and past forms of these irregular verbs with *a, e, i, o,* or *u.*

Base form	Past
1 beg_i_n	beg_a_n
2 c__me	c__me
3 dr__nk	dr__nk
4 dr__ve	dr__ve
5 g__ve	g__ve
6 kn__w	kn__w
7 p__t	p__t
8 s__t	s__t
9 sw__m	sw__m
10 w__ke [up]	w__ke [up]
11 w__n	w__n
12 wr__te	wr__te

b Complete the sentences with the simple past form of the verbs in the box.

buy find break hear make take can lose meet think

1 Last night we ___heard___ a noise downstairs.
2 They _____ the man's daughter was the murderer.
3 The police officer _____ the money in an old bag.
4 They _____ their friends outside the restaurant.
5 I _____ a detective story in the bookstore.
6 My wife _____ her cell phone last night.
7 The man _____ a window and went into the house.
8 Somebody _____ my laptop when I was out of the room.
9 We were worried because we _____ see a police car outside our house.
10 I was thirsty so I _____ a cup of tea.

3 PRONUNCIATION simple past verbs

a Match the verbs with the same vowel sound.

drove could ~~made~~ said learned bought had

1 came   ___made___
2 left   _____
3 ran   _____
4 saw   _____
5 spoke   _____
6 took   _____
7 heard   _____

b iChecker Listen and check. Then listen and repeat.

4 LISTENING

a iChecker Listen to a radio interview with a detective. What does he like most about his job?

_____

b iChecker Listen again and choose a, b, or c.

1 Jeremy Downs decided he wanted to be a detective...
   a when he was a child.
   b when he left school.
   c when he finished college.
2 His first job in the police was as...
   a a teacher.
   b a police officer.
   c a detective.
3 Jeremy took a ... to make sure he was strong and healthy for the job.
   a a law test
   b a running test
   c physical fitness
4 Jeremy usually works...
   a outside.
   b in an office.
   c at the police station.
5 He sometimes feels...when he is at work.
   a bored
   b stressed
   c worried

USEFUL WORDS AND PHRASES

Learn these words and phrases.

library /ˈlaɪbrɛri/
murder /ˈmərdər/
nobody /ˈnoʊbadi/
secretary /ˈsɛkrəteri/
believe /bɪˈliv/
kill /kɪl/
marry /ˈmæri/
business partner /ˈbɪznəs pɑrtnər/

8B A house with a history

1 GRAMMAR *there is / there are, some / any* + plural nouns

a Complete the dialogue with the correct form of *there is | there are* and, if necessary, *a*, *some*, or *any*.

A Hello. I'm interested in the apartment for rent.

B Oh, OK Let me tell you about it. ¹ ___There's a___ large living room and ² _____ small kitchen.

A ³ _____ table in the kitchen?

B No, ⁴ _____. But ⁵ _____ very nice dining room with a table and some chairs.

A That's fine. What about the bedrooms? How many bedrooms ⁶ _____?

B ⁷ _____ three bedrooms and a bathroom.

A ⁸ _____ shower in the bathroom?

B Yes, ⁹ _____.

A Good. ¹⁰ _____ bookshelves in the living room?

B No, I'm sorry. But ¹¹ _____ cupboards.

A That's OK. I think it's perfect for us. How much is it?

b Write the sentences in the plural using *some* or *any*.

1 There's an armchair in the living room.
   ___There are some armchairs in the living room___.

2 Is there a rug downstairs?
   _____?

3 There's a CD on the shelf.
   _____.

4 Is there a glass in the cupboard?
   _____?

5 There isn't a light in the study.
   _____.

c (Circle) the correct form.

¹(**It's**)/ **There's** a nice apartment and ² **it isn't** / **there isn't** very expensive. ³ **There are** / **They are** two rooms, but ⁴ **there aren't** / **they aren't** very big. ⁵ **There's** / **It is** a small kitchen and a bathroom. ⁶ **There isn't** / **It isn't** a bathtub in the bathroom, but ⁷ **it's** / **there's** a new shower. The apartment is on the 10th floor, so ⁸ **there's** / **it is** a great view of the city. And ⁹ **there's** / **it's** a very large balcony with a lot of flowers. ¹⁰ **They are** / **There are** beautiful in the summer!

2 VOCABULARY the house

a Complete the crossword.

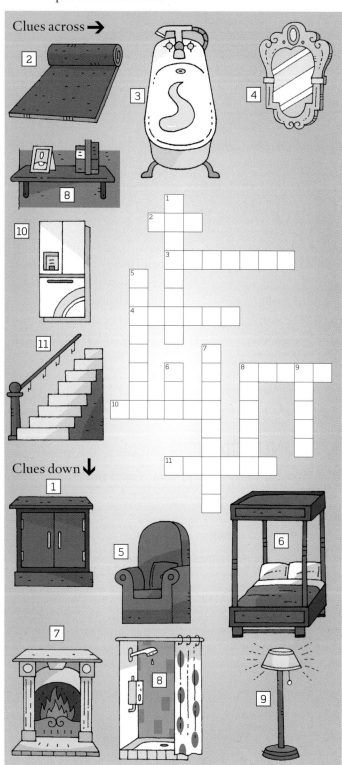

Clues across →

Clues down ↓

52

b Write the room.

1 You usually take off your coat in the h_all_.
2 You usually take a shower in the b_____.
3 You usually have dinner in the d_____
   r_____.
4 You usually use a computer in the st_____.
5 You usually park your car in the g_____.
6 You usually make lunch in the k_____.
7 You usually watch television in the l_____
   r_____.
8 You usually sleep in the b_____.
9 You usually sit outside in the y_____.

3 PRONUNCIATION /ɛr/ and /ɪr/; sentence stress

a (Circle) the word with a different sound.

 ɛr chair	1	they're	there	dear
 ɪr ear	2	cheers	stairs	near
 ɛr chair	3	where	wear	we're
 ɪr ear	4	here	hair	hear

b **iChecker** Listen and repeat the words.

c Underline the stressed syllable.

1 of|fice
2 mirr|or
3 cu|pboard
4 bal|co|ny
5 bath|tub
6 so|fa
7 arm|chair
8 ga|rage
9 cei|ling

d **iChecker** Listen and check. Then listen and repeat the words.

4 LISTENING

a **iChecker** Listen to Mrs. Goodings show her house to Bradley and Joanna, a couple who are interested in renting it. Check ✓ the **three** rooms Mrs. Goodings shows them.

1 bathroom ☐
2 bedroom ☐
3 dining room ☐
4 garage ☐
5 hall ☐
6 kitchen ☐
7 living room ☐
8 study ☐

b **iChecker** Listen again and write T (true) or F (false).

1 Mrs. Goodings always eats in the kitchen. _T_
2 Joanna doesn't like the living room. __
3 There isn't a washing machine in the kitchen. __
4 There's a hole in the ceiling of the kitchen. __
5 Joanna likes the windows in the living room. __
6 There isn't a TV in the living room. __
7 There are three bedrooms upstairs. __
8 Bradley forgets about the hole in the bathroom ceiling. __

USEFUL WORDS AND PHRASES

Learn these words and phrases.

advertisement /ˌædvərˈtaɪzmənt/
dishwasher /ˈdɪʃwɑʃər/
lovely /ˈlʌvli/
rent /rɛnt/
a long time ago /ə lɔŋ taɪm əˈgoʊ/
Wow! /waʊ/
How horrible! /haʊ ˈhɔrəbl/
It's perfect! /ɪts ˈpərfɪkt/

53

I'm not frightened of death.
I just don't want to be there when it happens.
Woody Allen, American movie director

8C A night in a haunted hotel

1 GRAMMAR *there was / there were*

a Complete the text. Use *was*, *were*, *wasn't*, or *weren't*.

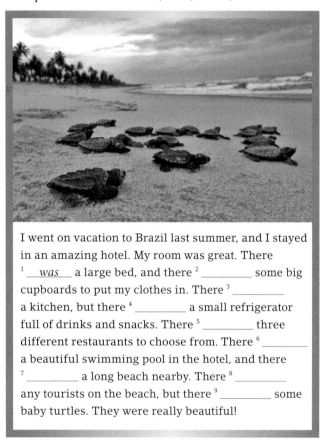

I went on vacation to Brazil last summer, and I stayed in an amazing hotel. My room was great. There ¹ _*was*_ a large bed, and there ² _____ some big cupboards to put my clothes in. There ³ _____ a kitchen, but there ⁴ _____ a small refrigerator full of drinks and snacks. There ⁵ _____ three different restaurants to choose from. There ⁶ _____ a beautiful swimming pool in the hotel, and there ⁷ _____ a long beach nearby. There ⁸ _____ any tourists on the beach, but there ⁹ _____ some baby turtles. They were really beautiful!

b Complete the dialogue with a form of *there was / there were*.

A Did you have a good vacation?
B Not really. ¹ _*There was*_ a problem with my hotel.
A Oh, no. What happened?
B Well, we couldn't swim because ² _____ a swimming pool. And ³ _____ any restaurants near the hotel.
A ⁴ _____ a small refrigerator in your room?
B No, ⁵ _____ a small refrigerator and ⁶ _____ a television. The only thing in my room was the bed!
A Oh. ⁷ _____ a bathroom?
B Yes, but ⁸ _____ any clean towels. Everything was very dirty.
A ⁹ _____ any nice people at the hotel?
B Yes, ¹⁰ _____ some great people, but they all felt the same as me – very angry!

2 VOCABULARY prepositions: place and movement

Complete the sentences with these words.

behind	from...to	in	in front of	next to
across from	out of	over	under	up

1 There's a family _*in*_ the dining room.
2 The boy is sitting _____ the girl.
3 The woman is _____ the man.
4 There's a ghost standing _____ the woman.
5 There's a bag _____ the table.
6 A waiter is coming _____ the kitchen.
7 There's a ghost _____ the waiter.
8 The waiter is carrying the plates _____ the kitchen _____ the tables.
9 There's a clock _____ the kitchen door.
10 A ghost is going _____ the stairs.

3 PRONUNCIATION silent letters

a ~~Cross out~~ the silent letters.

1 g̶host   3 white   5 hour   7 builder
2 cupboard   4 know   6 walk   8 wrong

b  Listen and repeat. <u>Copy</u> the <u>rhy</u>thm.

c  Listen and <u>underline</u> the stressed words.

1 There was a lamp on the table.
2 There wasn't a bathtub in the bathroom.
3 Was there a mirror in the bedroom?
4 There were some books on the shelf.
5 There weren't any cupboards in the kitchen.
6 Were there any plants in the study?

d  Listen again and repeat the sentences.

4 READING

Read the text. Write T (true) or F (false).

1 Maesmawr Hall is more than 500 years old.   *F*
2 People have seen ghosts inside and outside the hotel.   __
3 The ghosts are all of people who lived in the house in the past. __
4 Robin Drwg's ghost sometimes appears as a bull.   __
5 Paranormal investigators didn't think that Maesmawr Hall
   was haunted.   __

5 LISTENING

a  Listen to four people talking about hotel
rooms. Which countries did they visit?

_____

b  Listen again. Match the speakers to the rooms.

Speaker 1 ☐   Speaker 2 ☐   Speaker 3 ☐   Speaker 4 ☐

A The room was under the water.
B The room had mirrors on the walls and the ceiling.
C The room wasn't very comfortable.
D The room was up a tree.

USEFUL WORDS AND PHRASES

Learn these words and phrases.

ghosts /goʊsts/	haunted /ˈhɔntəd/
guest /gɛst/	strange /streɪndʒ/
owner /ˈoʊnər/	In the middle of the night
priest /prist/	/ɪn ðə mɪdl əv ðə ˈnaɪt/
brave /breɪv/	remote control /rɪmoʊt kənˈtroʊl/
frightened /ˈfraɪtnd/	

iChecker **TESTS** FILE 8

Maesmawr Hall:
A Haunted House in Wales

Maesmawr Hall is a manor house in Powys, Wales. It was built in 1535 and today is a 20-bedroom hotel and venue for weddings. It is famous because people say it is haunted.

Many guests say that they have seen ghosts. A businessman who stayed at the hotel said that when he looked out of the window, he saw hundreds of Roman soldiers marching. In fact, in Roman times there was a road that passed through the grounds of Maesmawr Hall. Other guests said they saw the ghosts of the Davies sisters who owned the hotel in the 1900s, and the ghost of an old housekeeper walking through a wall in the hall. But perhaps most frightening is the story that the ghost of an evil man named Robin Drwg haunts the woods around the hotel. Some people say that they have seen this ghost suddenly change into the shape of a bull.

Maesmawr was on a TV show about houses with ghosts called *Most Haunted*. The TV show hosts and investigators from the Mid Wales Paranormal (MWP) reported a lot of strange activity in the hall – seeing balls of light, feeling movements, and hearing unusual sounds. During the investigation, the floor in one of the upstairs rooms moved. The hotel's current owner, Nigel Humphryson, says he often hears voices and banging noises that he cannot explain.

So if you're interested in ghosts, why not stay here? But don't go outside at night unless you're feeling really brave!

9A What I ate yesterday

1 GRAMMAR countable / uncountable nouns; a / an, some / any

a What did Sarah and Martin buy when they went shopping yesterday? Write *a*, *an*, or *some* in the blanks.

1 *some* sausages
2 _____ lettuce
3 _____ eggs
4 _____ carrots
5 _____ jam
6 _____ orange
7 _____ pineapple
8 _____ potato chips
9 _____ cookies
10 _____ milk

b Write the sentences in the affirmative ⊞ or negative ⊟ form.

1 There's some cheese in the refrigerator.
⊟ There *isn't any cheese in the refrigerator* .

2 There are some strawberries in our garden.
⊟ There _____ .

3 I didn't have an egg for breakfast.
⊞ I _____ .

4 There isn't any sugar in my tea.
⊞ There _____ .

5 I didn't eat any snacks yesterday.
⊞ I _____ .

6 There weren't any sandwiches in the kitchen.
⊞ There _____ .

7 I bought a pineapple at the supermarket.
⊟ I _____ .

8 There was some bread in the cupboard.
⊟ There _____ .

c Complete the dialogue with *a*, *an*, *some*, or *any*.

A What do we need to buy for our dinner party? Let's make a list.
B Well, I want to make ¹ *a* lasagne, so we need ² _____ pasta and ³ _____ meat.
A Pasta...and meat. What about tomatoes? Are there ⁴ _____ tomatoes in the refrigerator?
B Let's look. There's ⁵ _____ onion, but there aren't ⁶ _____ tomatoes. Put those on the list, too.
A OK...tomatoes. Is there ⁷ _____ cheese?
B Yes, there's ⁸ _____ mozzarella cheese, so that's perfect.
A Let's have ⁹ _____ salad with the lasagna.
B OK. Then we need to buy ¹⁰ _____ lettuce.
A What about dessert? Is there ¹¹ _____ fruit?
B No, there isn't. Let's get ¹² _____ strawberries.

2 VOCABULARY food

a Complete the crossword.

Clues across →

Clues down ↓

b Write the words in the correct column.

apples bananas candy carrots chocolate cookies
mushrooms onions oranges peas pineapple
potatoes potato chips sandwiches strawberries

Vegetables	Snacks	Fruit
_____	_____	*apples*
_____	_____	_____
_____	_____	_____
_____	_____	_____
_____	_____	_____

3 PRONUNCIATION the letters *ea*

a (Circle) the word with a different sound.

i — tree	1	m**ea**t br**ea**kfast t**ea**
ɛ — egg	2	br**ea**d h**ea**lthy ice cr**ea**m
eɪ — train	3	**ea**t gr**ea**t st**ea**k

b iChecker Listen and check. Then listen and repeat the words.

4 READING

a Read the article and match the headings to the paragraphs.

> coconut water   popsicles   roast camel

b Read the article again. Write T (true) or F (false).

1 The Bedouin people eat roast camel on special occasions.   *T*
2 There are seven ingredients in the Bedouin meal.   __
3 Frank Epperson's drink froze because the weather was cold.   __
4 He sold his first ice pop when he was 29 years old.   __
5 According to the article, you can find coconut water in all coconuts.   __
6 Coconut water has a lot of sugar.   __

c Guess the meaning of the highlighted words. Check in your dictionary.

5 LISTENING

a iChecker Listen to four speakers talking about their favorite meal. Complete the meals.

Speaker 1   roast _____
Speaker 2   _____ tikka masala
Speaker 3   hot dog and _____
Speaker 4   sweet and sour tofu and _____

b iChecker Listen again. Match the speakers to the sentences.

Speaker 1   ☐   A I often eat it outside.
Speaker 2   ☐   B I always order rice with it.
Speaker 3   ☐   C I have it at a local restaurant.
Speaker 4   ☐   D I eat it when I visit my parents.

USEFUL WORDS AND PHRASES

Learn these words and phrases.

cream /krim/
dishes /dɪʃɪz/
ingredients /ɪnˈgridiənts/
popcorn /ˈpɑpkɔrn/
sauce /sɔs/
sweet corn /ˈswit kɔrn/
(food) to go /ˈtoʊ goʊ/
delicious /dɪˈlɪʃəs/
vegetarian /vɛdʒəˈtɛriən/

Three interesting food facts

1 _____

The Bedouin people, who live in the deserts of Africa, sometimes prepare a very big meal to celebrate weddings. The cook uses some eggs, some fish, some chickens, a sheep, and a camel to prepare it. He stuffs the fish with the eggs, the chickens with the fish, the sheep with the chickens, and the camel with the sheep. Then he cooks all the ingredients together in an enormous oven in the ground.

2 _____

It was an 11-year-old American boy who invented these. In 1905, the boy, Frank Epperson, wanted to make a drink. He put some soda powder in a cup of water and used a stick to mix it. Then he forgot about the drink and left it outside. That night it was very cold, so the mixture froze. Eighteen years later, he made some more of the frozen mixture and sold his first one at an amusement park. The British call them "ice pops."

3 _____

You can find this liquid in young fruit that is still green. People drank it in South-East Asia, Africa, and the Caribbean before it became popular as a health drink. Today, athletes drink it after playing sports. It is very good for you as it is low in fats and sugars. Doctors sometimes use it in an emergency because it is similar to human plasma.

Human beings are 70% water.
With some people, the rest is collagen.

Martin Mull, American actor and writer

9B White gold

1 GRAMMAR quantifiers: *how much / how many, a lot of*, etc.

a Complete the questions. Then complete the sentences.

How much salt do you put on your food?

Not much.

1 He *doesn't put much salt on his food*.

_____ _____ sugar do you put in your tea?

A lot.

2 He _____.

_____ _____ cookies do you eat?

Not many.

3 She _____.

_____ _____ candy do you buy?

A lot.

4 He _____.

_____ _____ exercise do you do?

Not much.

5 He _____.

_____ _____ cups of coffee do you drink?

None.

6 She _____.

b Read the information and write questions.

FOOD FACTS

There is .81 ounces of sugar in an orange.

There are about 125 calories in a banana.

There are about 18 oranges in a carton of orange juice.

There is .04 ounces of salt in a bowl of cereal.

There are twelve eggs in a carton.

There are 16 ounces of jam in a jar.

1 _How much sugar is there in an orange_ ?
Answer: .81 ounces.

2 _____ ?
Answer: About 125.

3 _____ ?
Answer: About 18.

4 _____ ?
Answer: .04 ounces.

5 _____ ?
Answer: twelve.

6 _____ ?
Answer: 16 ounces.

2 VOCABULARY food containers

a Unscramble the words to make food containers.

1 rja   _____jar_____
2 bxo   _____
3 rncoat   _____
4 gab   _____
5 cpeagka   _____
6 nca   _____
7 totble   _____

b Complete the sentences with a container from **a**.

1 She was thirsty, so she bought a __can__ of soda.
2 Do you need the scissors to open the _____ of juice?
3 He took the _____ of strawberry jam out of the cupboard.
4 There is a large _____ of potato chips on the table.
5 We always take a _____ of water when we go for a walk.
6 Ken feels sick because he ate a big _____ of cookies.
7 I gave her a _____ of chocolates to say thank you.

3 PRONUNCIATION /ʃ/ and /s/

a Circle the word with a different sound.

s snake	1 **s**ugar	**s**alad	**c**ereal
ʃ shower	2 **s**ure	fre**sh**	**s**alt
s snake	3 ri**c**e	**sh**opping	**sc**ience
ʃ shower	4 **sh**ort	informa**ti**on	**ce**nter

b **iChecker** Listen and check. Then listen and repeat the words.

c **iChecker** Listen and repeat the sentences.

1 She saw Susan standing outside the study.
2 Shawn said sorry for singing in the shower.
3 Steve puts six spoons of sugar on his cereal.
4 Sylvia spends Saturdays in the shopping center.

4 LISTENING

a **iChecker** Listen to the radio program about food groups. Complete the examples of the groups.

1 carbohydrates: bread, pasta, _____, potatoes
2 fruits and vegetables: apples, oranges, _____, carrots
3 protein: meat, _____
4 milk and dairy: _____, yogurt
5 fats and sugars: cake, _____, candy, chips

b **iChecker** Listen again. Fill in the blanks with one word.

1 Carbohydrates give us _____.
2 Fruits and vegetables contain important _____.
3 Protein helps our bodies to _____ and repair.
4 Milk and dairy are important for our bones and _____.
5 You should eat fats and sugars _____ or _____ a week.

9C Quiz night

1 GRAMMAR comparative adjectives

a Write the comparative forms of these adjectives in the correct circle.

> ~~bad~~ beautiful cheap dry sad difficult dirty
> cold far wet high hungry comfortable thin good

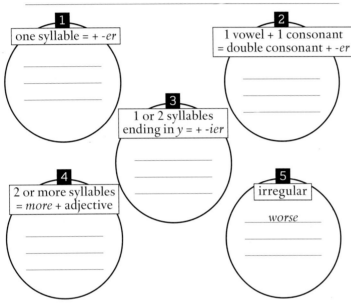

1 one syllable = + -er

2 1 vowel + 1 consonant = double consonant + -er

3 1 or 2 syllables ending in y = + -ier

4 2 or more syllables = *more* + adjective

5 irregular

worse

b Write sentences using the opposite adjective.

1 A bike is slower than a car.
A car *is faster than a bike* .

2 Lions are smaller than tigers.
Tigers _____ .

3 Brazil is wetter than Argentina.
Argentina _____ .

4 January is longer than February.
February _____ .

5 A laptop is more expensive than an iPod.
An iPod _____ .

6 Fridays are better than Mondays.
Mondays _____ .

7 A stove is hotter than a refrigerator.
A refrigerator _____ .

8 Spanish is easier than English.
English _____ .

2 VOCABULARY high numbers

a **iChecker** Listen and circle the correct numbers.

1	104	304
2	586	596
3	2,670	2,660
4	8,905	9,905
5	11,750	12,750
6	543, 830	553,830
7	1,315,000	1,350,000
8	25,460,000	35,460,000

b **iChecker** Listen and write the numbers in words.

1 125 _____
2 895 _____
3 4,500 _____
4 12,470 _____
5 33,930 _____
6 575,600 _____
7 6,250,000 _____
8 34,800,265 _____

3 PRONUNCIATION /ər/, sentence stress

a Write the words in the chart.

> ~~better~~ bigger cheaper colder dirtier drier easier
> healthier higher slower thinner worse

tr**ee**	f**i**sh	b**ir**d	**e**gg	ph**o**ne	b**i**ke
			better		

b **iChecker** Listen and repeat.

c iChecker Listen and underline the stressed words.

1 A pencil is cheaper than a pen.
2 China is bigger than Japan.
3 The kitchen is dirtier than the living room.
4 An apple is healthier than a cookie.
5 Canada is colder than Mexico.
6 Everest is higher than Kilimanjaro.

d iChecker Listen again and repeat the sentences. Copy the rhythm.

4 READING

a Read the sentences. Do you think they are T (true) or F (false)? Then read the article and check.

1 There are fewer car accidents on Tax Day. __
2 Elephants remember more than other animals. __
3 South America is bigger than North America. __
4 Margarine is healthier than butter. __

b Guess the meaning of the highlighted words. Check the meaning and pronunciation in your dictionary.

5 LISTENING

iChecker Listen to a conversation between a couple talking about two cities with the same name. Write T (true) or F (false).

1 More people live in Birmingham, UK than Birmingham, US. _T_
2 Birmingham, US is bigger than Birmingham, UK. __
3 Birmingham, US is greener than Birmingham, UK. __
4 Birmingham, US is older than Birmingham, UK. __
5 Birmingham, US is wetter than Birmingham, UK. __
6 Birmingham, US is hotter than Birmingham, UK. __

USEFUL WORDS AND PHRASES

Learn these words and phrases.

contestants /kənˈtɛstənts/
population /pɑpyəˈleɪʃn/
prize /praɪz/
approximately /əˈprɑksəmətli/
win a competition /wɪn ə kɑmpəˈtɪʃn/

---

iChecker TESTS FILE 9

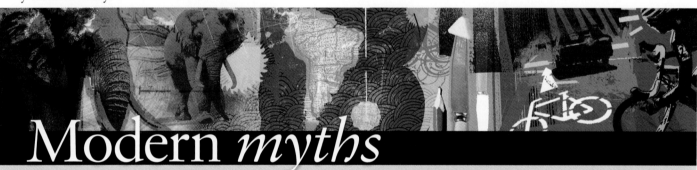

Modern *myths*

1 Elephants have brains that are bigger than any other land mammal. The expression "an elephant never forgets" suggests that the bigger an animal's brain is, the better that animal can remember things. Animal researchers discovered that this is actually true for elephants! These animals can remember details about areas of land as big as 1,200 square miles!

2 There are 12 countries in South America including Argentina and Brazil. It has an area of 6,888,062 square miles and its population is over 371,090,000. North America includes Canada and the US, but it also contains the countries of Central America. It covers an area of about 95,401,198 square miles, and its population is almost 529 million. This makes it bigger than South America.

3 When the *American Medical Association* studied the number of people injured in traffic accidents in the US, they got a surprise. They discovered that there were more dangerous car accidents on Tax Day. Tax Day is every year around April 15. People in the US are busy around this time!

4 Experts have different opinions about margarine and butter, and there is a big argument about which one is better for you. The truth is that margarine today is better than it was in the past because producers use a different type of vegetable oil. Butter still contains a lot of animal fat. Margarine today contains less fat which makes it healthier than butter.

1 VOCABULARY AND READING

a Look at the menu and answer the questions.

1 Which is the best appetizer for somebody on a diet?
2 What main course can a vegetarian have?
3 Can you have fruit for dessert?
4 How many types of coffee are there?
5 Do children pay the same as adults?

Taste of Heaven Restaurant
MENU

Appetizers
Chicken soup	$6.50
Shrimp cocktail	$9.25
Grilled vegetables with low-fat cheese (V)	$6.75

Salads
Tossed salad (V)	$5.50
Seafood salad	$7.25

Main courses
Roast beef served with roast potatoes and vegetables	$19.25
Mushroom risotto with Parmesan cheese (V)	$11.50
Grilled salmon served with French fries and peas	$16.75

Desserts
Fresh fruit salad	$6.95
Chocolate brownie with cream	$8.50
New York cheesecake	$8.25

Beverages
Iced tea	$2.75
Soda	$2.75
Coffee (espresso or latte)	$2.25

Today's specials
$19.95 (see the board for the daily specials)

25% discount on children's portions
(V) Suitable for vegetarians

b <u>Underline</u> the words or phrases you don't know. Use your dictionary to look up their meaning and pronunciation.

2 ORDERING A MEAL

Complete the dialogue with <u>one</u> word in each blank.

A Good evening. Do you have a ^{1} _reservation_ ?
B Yes, a ^{2} _____ for two. My name's Regina Morgan.
A Come this ^{3} _____, please.
A Are you ready to ^{4} _____?
B Yes. The grilled vegetables and the mushroom risotto, please.
C ^{5} _____ like the shrimp cocktail and then the roast beef, please.
A What would you ^{6} _____ to drink?
C ^{7} _____ water for me.
B A bottle of mineral water, please.
A ^{8} _____ or sparkling?
B Is sparkling OK?
C Yes, sparkling.
A Thank you, madam.
B Thank you.

3 SOCIAL ENGLISH

Match the sentences 1–6 to the correct responses a–f.

1 What do you do on your birthday? [c]
2 Would you like a dessert? [ ]
3 A decaf espresso. [ ]
4 Can I use your phone? [ ]
5 Good news? [ ]
6 Could we have the bill, please? [ ]

a Not for me, thanks.
b Yes. I got the job!
c ~~Nothing special.~~
d Yes, of course, sir.
e The same for me, please.
f Yes, go ahead.

As soon as there is life there is danger.

Ralph Waldo Emerson, American writer

10A The most dangerous road...

1 GRAMMAR superlative adjectives

a Complete the chart.

Adjective	Comparative	Superlative
1 cold	*colder*	*the coldest*
2 high		
3 expensive		
4 dry		
5 dangerous		
6 hot		
7 beautiful		
8 interesting		
9 good		
10 bad		

b Write the questions.

1 What / small continent / world
   What's the smallest continent in the world ?
2 What / big ocean / world
   _____ ?
3 What / large country / world
   _____ ?
4 What / populated city / world
   _____ ?
5 What / wet place / world
   _____ ?
6 What / dry desert / world
   _____ ?
7 What / common native language / world
   _____ ?
8 What / cold place / world
   _____ ?

c Circle the correct answer to the questions in **b**.

1 a Australia
  b Europe
  c South America
2 a The Atlantic
  b The Pacific
  c The Indian Ocean

3 a Canada
  b China
  c Russia
4 a Mumbai
  b Shanghai
  c Buenos Aires
5 a India
  b Ireland
  c Brazil
6 a The Sahara Desert (Africa)
  b The Painted Desert (The US)
  c The Atacama Desert (South America)
7 a Mandarin Chinese
  b English
  c Hindi
8 a The Arctic
  b Alaska
  c The Antarctic

2 VOCABULARY places and buildings

a Complete the sentences with a word in each box.

art department parking police post shopping town train

gallery hall lot mall office station station store

1 Where can you visit different stores?
  At a *shopping mall* .
2 Where can you see paintings?
  In an _____ _____.
3 Where can you get a train from?
  From a _____ _____.
4 Where can you buy a stamp?
  At a _____ _____.
5 Where can you talk to a police officer?
  At a _____ _____.
6 Where can you buy clothes for all the family?
  At a _____ _____.
7 Where can you leave your car?
  At a _____ _____.
8 Where can you speak to a local politician?
  In the _____ _____.

b Complete the puzzle. Can you find the hidden word?

3 PRONUNCIATION consonant groups

iChecker Listen and repeat the sentences.

1　It's the cheapest place to live.
2　It's the highest mountain in the world.
3　He's the healthiest person in the family.
4　It's the prettiest town in the country.
5　It's the most difficult language to learn.
6　It's the most polluted city in the area.
7　They're the most attractive couple I know.
8　She's the most intelligent person in the class.

4 LISTENING

a　**iChecker** Listen to a radio interview with a travel writer. What is his book called? _____

b　**iChecker** Listen again. Complete the sentences.

1　Uluru is the _____ rock in the world.
2　It's _____ feet long.
3　The world's highest waterfall is in _____.
4　The tallest building in the world is _____ feet high.
5　The world's oldest city began in _____ BC.
6　The world's longest train track goes from _____ to Vladivostok.
7　The shortest runway in the world is _____ feet long.

5 READING

a Read the text and write T (true) or F (false).

1　Ulm Münster is the world's biggest church. ___
2　You can sometimes see the mountains from the top of the church. ___
3　Ulm Münster was the city's first church. ___
4　Construction of the church took over 500 years. ___
5　The church opens every day at 8 o'clock. ___
6　It's very expensive to visit Ulm Münster. ___

b Guess the meaning of the highlighted words. Check in your dictionary.

THE SKY'S THE LIMIT

Ulm Münster in Germany is the tallest church in the world. The tallest part of the church is the steeple, which is 528 feet high and contains 768 steps. From the top of the church there is a view of the city, and on a clear day you can see the Alps.

Before the Münster was built, Ulm already had a church outside the city walls. However, the inhabitants of the city decided that they wanted a new church in the town center, and they agreed to pay for the building.

Construction of the church began in 1377, but the building wasn't completed until May 31, 1890. At first, the work was difficult because the heaviest parts fell down and the builders had to repair them. Then construction stopped from 1543 to 1817 for political reasons.

Today, tourists can visit the church every day of the year. In the winter, the church is open from 9 a.m. to 4:45 p.m. and the church is open in the summer months from 8 a.m. to 7:45 p.m. Admission to the church is free, but the price of climbing the steeple is €3 for adults and €2 for children.

USEFUL WORDS AND PHRASES

Learn these words and phrases.

accidents /ˈæksədənts/
fun /fʌn/
region /ˈridʒən/
almost /ˈɔlmoʊst/
popular /ˈpɑpyələr/
wide (*opposite* narrow) /waɪd/
below (*opposite* above) /bɪˈloʊ/

10B CouchSurf around the world!

1 GRAMMAR *be going to* (plans), future time expressions

a Order the words to make sentences.

1 are / there / you / get / to / How / going
   _How are you going to get there_____?

2 to / isn't / He / a / going / stay / in / hotel
   _____.

3 show / to / They're / city / going / the / me
   _____.

4 good / going / time / have / We're / to / a
   _____.

5 is / home / to / she / going / When / go
   _____?

6 not / sights / going / I'm / see / the / to
   _____.

b Complete the sentences. Use the correct form of *going to*.

1 _Are they going to leave_ by train? (they / leave)
2 We _____ our friends the city. (show)
3 They _____ nice meals in expensive restaurants. (have)
4 _____ with a friend? (you / stay)
5 They _____ the museum. (not visit)
6 _____ the sights? (they / see)
7 He _____ a lot of people. (meet)
8 She _____ on vacation this year. (not go)

c Complete the dialogue. Use the correct form of *going to*.

A So, where ¹ _are you going to go_ (go) on vacation?
B I ² _____ (travel) around the US for a few weeks.
A Really? Where ³ _____ (stay)?
B Well, this year I ⁴ _____ (not/sleep) in hotels. Instead, I'm going to CouchSurf.
A CouchSurf? What a great idea! ⁵ _____ (travel) alone?
B Yes, I am. My best friend ⁶ _____ (drive) to San Diego with some friends. They ⁷ _____ (spend) all day on the beach, and they ⁸ _____ (dance) all night. I don't like that kind of vacation. I ⁹ _____ (meet) a lot of new people and see a lot of new places.
A Which states ¹⁰ _____? (visit)
B Virginia first, and then North Carolina, South Carolina, and Georgia. My CouchSurfing hosts ¹¹ _____ (show) me the sights. I ¹² _____ (have) a great time!

2 VOCABULARY vacations

a Write the expressions in the correct column.

~~back home~~   by train   a good time   on vacation
the sights   in a hotel   nice meals
somebody around your town   with a friend

GO	*back home*
HAVE	
SEE	
SHOW	
STAY	

b Complete the text with the verbs from **a**.

Maria is really happy because she's going to ¹ _go_ on vacation tomorrow. She's going to ² _____ with her cousins in Buenos Aires. They're going to ³ _____ her around the city, and she's going to ⁴ _____ all the sights. They're going to ⁵ _____ a lot of nice meals together. She's going to ⁶ _____ by plane, and she's going to ⁷ _____ in Buenos Aires for a week. The second week, Maria and her cousins are going to travel to the coast. They're going to ⁸ _____ in a hotel, and they're going to ⁹ _____ a great time. Maria's going to ¹⁰ _____ back to Buenos Aires before she goes home.

3 PRONUNCIATION sentence stress

a **iChecker** Listen and <u>underline</u> the stressed words.

1 How are you going to get there?
2 Where are you going to stay?
3 We're going to stay for a week.
4 I'm going to see the sights.
5 We aren't going to go by car.
6 I'm not going to stay in a hotel.

b **iChecker** Listen again and repeat the sentences. Copy the <u>rhythm</u>.

4 LISTENING

a **iChecker** Listen to four speakers talking about their first experience CouchSurfing. How many people did <u>not</u> enjoy the experience? _____

b **iChecker** Listen again and match the speakers to the sentences A–D.

Speaker 1 ☐   Speaker 3 ☐
Speaker 2 ☐   Speaker 4 ☐

A CouchSurfing gave me the chance to make friends.
B CouchSurfing helped me with my work.
C My host was also my tour guide to the city.
D My second experience CouchSurfing was better than the first.

5 READING

a Read the text. Answer the questions with **A** (Angela), **J** (Jay), **S** (Sofia), or **T** (Tomo).

1 Which person made new friends while traveling? ☐
2 Who spent very little on accomodations? ☐
3 Who used his or her InterRail pass on another form of transportation? ☐
4 Who was traveling abroad for the first time? ☐
5 Which person found it easy to make new plans while traveling? ☐

USEFUL WORDS AND PHRASES

Learn these words and phrases.

couch /kaʊtʃ/
roommate /ˈrʊmmeɪt/
a host /ə ˈhoʊst/
create a profile /kriˈeɪt ə ˈproʊfaɪl/
recommend (things to do) /rɛkəˈmɛnd/
Have a good trip! /hæv ə gʊd ˈtrɪp/
It's free. /ɪts ˈfri/
Things didn't work out. /θɪŋz ˈdɪdnt wərk aʊt/

Traveling by InterRail

Since 1972, backpackers have enjoyed the freedom to explore 30 European countries thanks to the InterRail pass. Here, InterRail travelers say why they love InterRail so much.

Angela Bowman, (23, the US)

Route
Amsterdam – Hamburg – Berlin – Warsaw – Krakow – Prague – Vienna – Budapest – Zagreb – Split – Mostar – Sarajevo – Belgrade

I love InterRail because you can go where you want, when you want! When we started our trip, we had an idea of where we wanted to go, but as we traveled, we got new ideas. Changing our plans was easy – you can stay an extra night or two if you like a place, and if you don't like it, you can go somewhere else. The InterRail pass gives you real freedom.

Jay Honahan (26, Canada)

Route
Amsterdam – Bonn – Stuttgart – Salzburg – Ljubljana – Split – Pescara – Bari – Corfu – Igoumenitsa – Patras – Athens

One of the best things about InterRail is that you get cheaper, or even free travel on ferries as well as trains. I traveled to Split in Croatia and then took the ferry to Pescara in Italy. Then I traveled by InterRail to the south of Italy and then took the ferry to the Greek island of Corfu. It was fantastic! You also get discounts on hotels, tourist attractions, and a lot more.

Sofia Valenzuela (26, Mexico)

Route
Paris – Versailles – Épernay – Blois – Angers – Lyons – Chamonix – Nice – Monaco – Ventimiglia – Pisa – Florence – Perugia – Assisi – Rome – Naples

In six weeks, I met so many new, interesting people and made friends from all over the world. It's a cheap way to travel too, especially if you take the night trains – I saved a lot of money on accomodations this way. I really want to go InterRailing again!

Tomo Nagasaki (21, Japan)

Route
Innsbruck – Venice – Sienna – Lucca – Pisa – Florence – Cannes – Monaco – Nice – Figueras – Rosas – Barcelona – Paris – Antwerp

This was the first time I'd left Japan, and I loved it. InterRail is safe and easy for first-time travelers. I got an InterRail Global Pass so I could take as many trains as I wanted. I saw many amazing places, and learned a lot about Europe's culture and history. I visited over 15 cities in less than a month. I'm definitely going to do it again next year!

10C What's going to happen?

1 GRAMMAR *be going to* (predictions)

a Look at the pictures. Write sentences using these verbs and *be going to*.

buy change ~~eat~~ have listen lose read take

1 *They're going to eat* a pizza.
2 _____ some money.
3 _____ a newspaper.
4 _____ a coffee.
5 _____ to music.
6 _____ a book.
7 _____ a photo.
8 _____ his passport.

b Write a letter in the box: **A** = plan, **B** = prediction.

1 I'm going to buy some stamps. [A]
2 It's going to be cold tomorrow. [ ]
3 Jim's going to study tonight. [ ]
4 Our team is going to lose this game. [ ]
5 There's going to be a storm later. [ ]
6 I think that restaurant's going to close. [ ]
7 They're going to buy a new TV. [ ]
8 I'm going to book a flight online. [ ]

2 VOCABULARY verb phrases

Complete the phrases with verbs from the box.

~~be~~ become fall get (x3) ~~have~~ meet move travel

1 *be* lucky
2 _____ somebody new
3 _____ to a different country
4 _____ married
5 _____ a lot of money
6 _____ in love
7 _____ famous
8 _____ a new job
9 *have* a surprise
10 _____ to a new house

3 PRONUNCIATION the letters *oo*

a Look at the pairs of words. Check ✓ the pairs with the same sound and put an ✗ on the pairs that are different.

1 choose	school	✓
2 book	soon	✗
3 food	moon	
4 good	cook	
5 took	spoon	
6 look	too	

b **iChecker** Listen and check. Then listen and repeat.

4 READING

a Read the text. Match the headings to the paragraphs.

1 Give me your hand   3 How do you like your tea?
2 Let's play cards   4 What's inside the ball?

b Read the text again and write T (true) or F (false).

1 The easiest way to read tarot cards is to use four cards.   —
2 An image of a nurse means bad health.   —
3 A strong heart line means you're going to find love.   —
4 A shape of a bird means bad luck.   —

c Guess the meaning of the highlighted words. Check in your dictionary.

5 LISTENING

a **iChecker** Listen to Pete and Amy's conversation about the psychic Uri Geller. Was his trick with the spoons real?

_____

b **iChecker** Listen again and write T (true) or F (false).

1 A lot of people watched Uri Geller in the past.   —
2 Pete and Amy see a video of the trick.   —
3 Amy doesn't believe the trick at first.   —
4 Uri doesn't use a normal spoon.   —
5 Uri doesn't speak during the trick.   —
6 Today, Uri doesn't appear in public.   —

The name behind the method

A _____

In tasseography, *the fortune-teller uses tea leaves to predict the future. You drink a cup of tea and leave a small amount in the bottom of the cup. Then you move the tea around the cup three times, cover it with a* saucer, *and turn it* upside down. *The fortune-teller looks at the shape the tea leaves make. For example, a bird means that you're going to have good news.*

B _____

In crystallomancy, *the fortune-teller uses a glass ball. She places the ball on the table between you and her, and looks into it for a long period of time. At first, the ball looks* dull *and cloudy, but then it clears and images start to appear. The fortune-teller uses these pictures to predict your future. For example, a nurse means that you're going to be sick.*

C _____

In tarot reading, *the fortune-teller uses a special pack of tarot cards to predict the future. There are 78 cards in the pack, and there are different ways of using them. The quickest is to lay three cards on the table from left to right. The cards represent the past, the present, and the future. The fortune-teller turns over the cards and says what they mean. For example, the sun means that you're going to become famous.*

D _____

Chiromancy is also called palmistry *and it's when the fortune-teller studies the lines on the* palm *of your hand to predict your future. There are four major lines on the hand: the life line, the head line, the* heart *line, and the health line. For example, a strong heart line means that you're going to find the right partner and be happy in your life.*

USEFUL WORDS AND PHRASES

Learn these words and phrases.

soon /sun/
be lucky /bi ˈlʌki/
Come in! /kʌm ɪn/
get married /gɛt ˈmærid/
move to another country /muv tu ənʌðər ˈkʌntri/

iChecker **TESTS** FILE 10

You can fall in love at first sight with a place as with a person.

Alec Waugh, British writer

11A First impressions

1 GRAMMAR adverbs (manners and modifiers)

a Complete the sentences with an adverb.

1 The French cook perfect meals.
 They cook ___*perfectly*___ .
2 The Americans are careful drivers.
 They drive _____ .
3 The British are very polite.
 They speak very _____ .
4 The Brazilians are good at soccer.
 They play soccer _____ .
5 The Japanese are very hard workers.
 They work very _____ .
6 The Canadians eat healthy food.
 They eat _____ .
7 The Argentinians are beautiful dancers.
 They dance _____ .

b Circle the correct word.

1 My brother dresses **casual** / **casually** .
2 Shoji cooks **real** / **really** well.
3 It's **easy** / **easily** to ride a bike.
4 They walked **quick** / **quickly** to the train station.
5 He's very **quiet** / **quietly** . He never says anything!
6 Elena's pizzas are **incredible** / **incredibly** .
7 My French is very **bad** / **badly** .
8 Can you speak more **slow** / **slowly** ?
9 Mark speaks English **good** / **well** .
10 She eats **unhealthily** / **unhealthy** .
11 They have **real** / **really** stressful jobs.

2 VOCABULARY common adverbs

Make adverbs from the adjectives and complete the sentences.

careful good easy hard healthy incredible perfect quiet

In the ideal city...

1 ...car drivers drive ___*carefully*___ .
2 ...workers work _____ .
3 ...families eat _____ .
4 ...people speak foreign languages _____ .
5 ...you can travel around _____ .
6 ...people talk _____ .
7 ...everybody treats tourists _____ .
8 ...everything is _____ cheap.

3 PRONUNCIATION word stress

a Underline the stressed syllable in the adverbs. Which **three** adverbs are <u>not</u> stressed on the first syllable?

_____ , _____ , _____

1 beau|ti|ful|ly
2 care|ful|ly
3 ca|su|al|ly
4 dan|ge|rous|ly
5 fa|shio|na|bly
6 in|cre|di|bly
7 per|fect|ly
8 po|lite|ly
9 un|heal|thi|ly

b **iChecker** Listen and check. Then listen and repeat the adverbs.

4 READING

a Read the text. Match the headings A-D to the paragraphs.

A The Mexican way of life
B Feeling at home abroad
C My first impressions
D Not what I expected

First impressions of Mexico City

Christina Hornick, from the US, came to Mexico for the first time three years ago. She now lives in Mexico City where she is a teacher.

1 _____

You always remember your first impressions of a new country. When I first came to Mexico City, I didn't know much about Mexico at all. I didn't know anything about the culture. I didn't think the food was very different from American food, and I expected the weather to be similar to North Carolina in the US—maybe even warmer! But when I got there, I discovered how wrong I was.

2 _____

It was summer, and it was warm, but not hot. In fact, the temperature was about 70 degrees Fahrenheit. My first impression was that Mexico City was more beautiful than I expected. I spent a lot of time looking at the incredible architecture. The city was so colorful and had a wonderful atmosphere. I saw pink, yellow, and red houses. The trees were colorful too with pink and purple flowers.

3 _____

Mexican people are very friendly. A lot of Mexicans can speak a little English, and some speak it very well. I speak Spanish pretty well, but when I make a mistake, my Mexican friends don't mind. Mexican people are very hospitable and they love to socialize —get together, eat, dance, and play music. At parties, there is often a lot of delicious, homemade food to eat. And there is often very loud music which makes it hard to hear people!

4 _____

Mexico is a great place to live. It has everything—friendly people, great public transportation, and delicious food. In Mexico City, the summers are warm, and the winters are cool. It's great weather for long walks in the nearby canyons. Mexico has mountains, lakes, beaches, and rivers. It has many beautiful cities and a fascinating culture. I still love the US, but Mexico feels like home now.

b Complete the sentences with words in the box.

atmosphere	culture	socializing	fascinating
hospitality	architecture	expect	

1 Before she went to Mexico City, Christina didn't know much about Mexican _____.
2 She didn't _____ the city to be so beautiful.
3 She was very impressed by the _____ in Mexico City.
4 She liked the colors and the wonderful _____ of the city.
5 The _____ of the Mexican people is warm and welcoming.
6 Mexican people like _____ with their friends and family.
7 Christina finds the Mexican culture _____ .

c Guess the meaning of the highlighted words. Check with your dictionary.

5 LISTENING

iChecker Listen to two people talking about where they live. Answer the questions.

Speaker 1   Toronto, Canada

1 Where don't people usually go on the weekends?
2 How do people normally dress during the week?
3 Why is Toronto's nickname "Hollywood North?"

Speaker 2   Reykjavik, Iceland

4 When do people go to swimming pools and hot tubs?
5 What are there very few of in the Icelandic countryside?
6 How many people are there…?
   in Reykjavik
   in the second-biggest city
7 What kind of things do Icelandic people make?

USEFUL WORDS AND PHRASES

Learn these words and phrases.

a foreigner   /ˈfɔrənər/
myth   /mɪθ/
subtitles   /ˈsʌbtaɪtlz/
incredible   /ɪnˈkrɛdəbl/
incredibly   /ɪnˈkrɛdəbli/
dress (well)   /ˈdrɛs/
a strong accent   /ə strɔŋ ˈæksɛnt/
first impressions   /fərst ɪmˈprɛʃnz/
get dark   /gɛt ˈdɑrk/
in general   /ɪn ˈdʒɛnərəl/
lock (your) doors   /lɑk ˈdɔrz/

11B What do you want to do?

1 GRAMMAR verb + infinitive

a Complete the sentences with *to* and a verb in the box.

become cook download go ride spend
stop visit

1 I'd like ___to go___ on a safari.
2 My brother's learning _____ a motorcycle.
3 Do you need _____ less time on your computer?
4 She wants _____ biting her nails.
5 Would you like _____ New York City?
6 We know all their songs, so we don't need _____ the lyrics.
7 I'm leaving home next month so I need to learn _____ a meal.
8 Do you want _____ a singer?

b Write sentences or questions with *would like*. Use contractions.

1 he / have very long hair −
   ___He wouldn't like to have very long hair___ .
2 you / climb a mountain ?
   _____
   _____ ?
3 we / get up earlier +
   _____
   _____ .
4 I / learn to fly a plane +
   _____
   _____ .
5 she / make a short movie −
   _____
   _____ .
6 they / get married ?
   _____
   _____ ?

2 VOCABULARY verbs that take the infinitive

Match the sentences 1–8 with the sentences a–h.

1 I'm taking some lessons. ☑ *f*
2 Our washing machine is broken. ☐
3 I have a lot of dresses. ☐
4 I'm playing tennis tomorrow. ☐
5 That girl is Brazilian so I can't speak to her. ☐
6 We are looking at hotels in Miami, Florida. ☐
7 I don't have time to do my homework now. ☐
8 I love Carrie Underwood and her music. ☐

a I'd like to learn Portuguese.
b I promise to do it later.
c I hope to win the match.
d I want to get tickets to her concert.
e We're planning to go there on vacation.
f ~~I'm learning to drive.~~
g We need to buy a new one.
h I decided to wear the red one.

3 PRONUNCIATION sentence stress

a Underline the stressed words.

1 **A** Would you like to drive a sports car?
  B Yes, I'd love to.
  A Why?
  B Because I love cars, and I love driving.
2 **A** Would you like to ride a horse?
  B No, I wouldn't.
  A Why not?
  B Because I don't like horses.
3 **A** Do you want to learn to cook?
  B Yes, I need to.
  A Why?
  B Because I want to live on my own.

b **iChecker** Listen and check. Then listen and repeat the dialogues.

4 LISTENING

a **iChecker** Listen to a TV host interviewing three people about things they want to do with their lives. What are their ambitions?

1 Dave _____

2 Carolina _____

3 Eddie _____

b **iChecker** Listen again and write T (true) or F (false).

1 Dave had a bicycle when he was younger. —
2 Dave isn't a father. —
3 Carolina is planning to visit Canada with her sister. —
4 Carolina enjoys flying. —
5 Eddie has tickets to see his favorite band in concert. —
6 Kings of Leon isn't touring this year. —

---

5 READING

a Read the text. Answer the questions with **J** (Julio), **K** (Kimberley), **Y** (Yusuke), or **G** (Greg).

Things I want to do

Julio, 25, Brazil

I'd love to be in Times Square in New York City at midnight on New Year's Eve! And I'd like it to be snowing, too – that's more romantic. People say that the atmosphere there is amazing. I think it would be a great experience.

Kimberly, 31, Canada

I want to visit the Amazon rainforest. It's such a unique and fascinating place, and I'm really interested in the wildlife that lives there. I'd like to do a trek and go camping there for three weeks or so. I've seen a lot of movies about explorers, and now I'd like to do something really exciting myself.

Yusuke, 26, Japan

What I want to do is go on a road trip across Europe with my two best friends. I've been to the US and Canada, but I've never been to Europe. I want to see all the famous tourist sites like the Eiffel Tower, Big Ben, and the Leaning Tower of Pisa. I read about them in books when I was a child – it would be a dream come true for me to see them in real life.

Greg, 34, the US

It's not very original, but I'd like to drive a really expensive sports car up the coast of California with my wife next to me in the passenger seat. However, right now I own a Toyota Corolla, so I may have to wait a few years before I can achieve my dream!

1 Which person became interested in his or her dream when he or she was very young? ☐
2 Who wants to be part of a traditional celebration? ☐
3 Who needs to buy something before he or she can achieve his or her dream? ☐
4 Which person would like some adventure? ☐

b Guess the meaning of the highlighted words. Check the meaning and pronunciation in your dictionary.

11C Men, women, and the Internet

1 GRAMMAR articles

a Correct the mistake in each answer (**B**).

1 **A** Where are the children?   **B** They're at ~~the~~ school.
2 **A** What do you do?   **B** I'm engineer.
3 **A** Where's the juice?   **B** In a refrigerator.
4 **A** What's that?   **B** A ID card.
5 **A** How often do you go?   **B** Twice the week.
6 **A** What animals do you like?   **B** I like the dogs.
7 **A** How did you travel?   **B** By a train.
8 **A** Where did you get that?   **B** On Internet.

b Complete the text with *the*, *a* / *an*, or –.

Most people think that ¹ ___the___ Internet is a good thing. At ² _____ work, employees can use it to search for ³ _____ information and to send and receive ⁴ _____ emails. At ⁵ _____ home, ⁶ _____ people can use it for entertainment. You can watch ⁷ _____ music videos, listen to ⁸ _____ music, or, play ⁹ _____ latest computer games online. It is also useful for ¹⁰ _____ shopping, and you don't have to go to ¹¹ _____ bank if you have ¹² _____ online banking service. However, there are some dangers because there is ¹³ _____ problem with security. ¹⁴ _____ computer virus can break your computer and ¹⁵ _____ computer hackers can steal your identity.

2 VOCABULARY The Internet

Unscramble the words to complete the sentences.

1 All our hotel rooms have ___wi-fi___ (IW-IF) access.
2 It's cheaper to _____ (PKSEY) than to make a phone call.
3 Do you ever shop _____ (NONELI)?
4 You only need your username and your password to _____ (GOL NI).
5 Do you want to _____ (DLWODNAO) this file?
6 I sometimes forget to include the _____ (TATHCANEMT) in my emails.
7 I need to _____ (RASHEC ROF) some information before I write my report.
8 You can _____ (OGLEGO) the name of the restaurant to find out the address.
9 They're going to _____ (POLUDA) their vacation pictures tonight.

3 PRONUNCIATION word stress

a Underline the stressed syllable in these words.

1 email   network   website
2 address   online   results
3 document   Internet   username
4 attachment   computer   directions

b **iChecker** Listen and check. Then listen and repeat the words.

4 READING

a Read the article. When did the World Wide Web begin? _____

b Read the article again and number the events in the order they happened.

- [ ] Tim Berners-Lee developed a new computer language.
- [ ] Americans opened an agency to develop new technology.
- [ ] They put the new language on the Internet.
- [1] The Russians sent a satellite into space.
- [ ] The World Wide Web made the Internet available to all computer users.
- [ ] The network changed its name to the Internet.
- [ ] The agency developed a network to connect computers.
- [ ] Berners-Lee and a colleague used the new language to write a new program.

5 LISTENING

a  Listen to four speakers talking about how they use the Internet. Match speakers 1–4 to the thing they do most often.

Speaker [ ] uses a social network.
Speaker [ ] plays games.
Speaker [ ] does a job.
Speaker [ ] talks to family and friends.

b iChecker Listen again and match the speakers to the sentences A–D.

Speaker 1 [ ]   Speaker 3 [ ]
Speaker 2 [ ]   Speaker 4 [ ]

A This person often puts photos on the Internet.
B This person likes his / her job.
C This person uses the Internet to relax.
D This person saves money because of the Internet.

USEFUL WORDS AND PHRASES

Learn these words and phrases.

advice /ədˈvaɪs/
both /bəʊθ/
password /ˈpæswərd/
username /ˈyuzərneɪm/
book (tickets / hotels) /bʊk/
lose weight /luz ˈweɪt/
make transfers /meɪk ˈtrænsfərz/
online shopping /ɑnlaɪn ˈʃɑpɪŋ/
pay bills /peɪ ˈbɪlz/

The story behind the World Wide Web

To find out when the World Wide Web began, we first need to look at the Internet. The origins of the Internet go back to the space race of the 1950s. After the Russians sent the satellite *Sputnik* into space, Americans wanted to develop their own technology further, so they set up ARPA – the Advanced Research Projects Agency. This agency found a way of connecting computers, which they called ARPANET. In 1974, they changed its name to the internetwork or Internet for short.

In 1980, a scientist at CERN, the European Organization for Nuclear Research, wrote a computer program so that he and his colleagues could share their research. The scientist's name was Tim Berners-Lee, and his software was called ENQUIRE. At first, only scientists at CERN could use the program, which contained a new computer language called hypertext. Then, in 1991, he and a colleague wrote a more advanced version of the program which made hypertext available over the Internet. This was the beginning of the World Wide Web, as we know it. The first website and web server was info.cern.ch. Today, there are more than 227 million websites containing over 65 billion web pages.

Over two billion people now use the Internet, which is nearly a third of the world's population.

Practical English Going home

1 VOCABULARY Public transportation

Complete the paragraphs.

1 You can get a taxi or a ¹ _cab_ at a taxi
² s_____. People usually give
the driver a ³ t_____.

2 Before you get a plane, you have to
⁴ ch_____ in online or at the airport.
Then you go through security to the
⁵ d_____ area. Finally, you
go to your ⁶ g_____.

3 You get a subway at a subway ⁷ st_____.
First, you get a ⁸ t_____, and then
you find the right ⁹ pl_____.

4 You get a ¹⁰ b_____ at a station
or a stop. You can buy a ticket in advance
or sometimes you can pay
the ¹¹ dr_____.

2 GETTING TO THE AIRPORT

Complete the conversations with a sentence in the box.

Can I pay by credit card?
~~Could you call me a taxi, please?~~
Could I have a ticket to O'Hare Airport, please?
How much is it?   And could I have a receipt?
Now, please.   One-way, please.
Coach, please.   To Union Station.

1 A ¹ _Could you call me a taxi, please?_
   B Yes, of course. Where to?
   A ²_____
   B And when would you like it for?
   A ³_____

2 A ⁴_____
   C That's $18.50, please.
   A Make it $20. ⁵_____
   C Yes, of course. Thank you very much, sir.

3 A ⁶_____
   D One-way or round-trip?
   A ⁷_____
   D Coach or first class?
   A ⁸_____
   D That's $18.50.
   A ⁹_____
   D Yes, of course.

3 SOCIAL ENGLISH

Match the words to make phrases.

1 I can't	_e_	a to accept.
2 Thank you	☐	b good trip.
3 I'd love	☐	c in Rio de Janeiro.
4 I'm so	☐	d so much.
5 Have a	☐	e ~~believe it!~~
6 See you	☐	f happy.

4 READING

a Read the text about O'Hare International Airport.

O'Hare International Airport

O'Hare International Airport is the second-busiest international airport in the US, and more than 32 million passengers pass through it every year. Below you can find different ways of getting to the airport.

BY CAR
If you're planning to drive to O'Hare Airport, you need to take Interstate I-190 and turn off on Bessie Coleman Drive. The airport is 19 miles from downtown Chicago and takes about 35 minutes during quiet times.

BY BIKE
Ride your bike to O'Hare Airport's Parking Lot E. You can leave your bike in a special bike parking area in this parking lot. Then take the Airport Transit System (ATS) to the terminal buildings.

BY TRAIN
Chicago Transit Authority's Blue Line runs every ten minutes. It takes about an hour to go from Forest Park to O'Hare Airport. A one-way ticket costs $2.25. Students and senior citizens can ride for a reduced price.

BY BUS
Several different bus companies around Chicago operate services to O'Hare Airport. These buses run 24 hours a day and drop you off in front of the terminal buildings. The price for a one-way ticket can be as low as just a few dollars.

BY TAXI
There are more than 15 different taxi companies to call for a ride to O'Hare Airport. The cost of a taxi from downtown Chicago to the airport is about $45, and the trip takes about 30 to 45 minutes depending on traffic.

b How did the following people get to O'Hare Airport?

1 Diego made a phone call.   By _taxi_____.
2 Vanessa paid $2.25.   By _____.
3 Samantha went from Forest Park. By _____.
4 Pete went on the Interstate.   By _____.
5 Yoshi exercised.   By _____.

c Underline five words or phrases you don't know. Use your dictionary to look up their meaning and pronunciation.

12A Books and movies

Films should have a beginning, a middle, and an end
– but not necessarily in that order.

Jean-Luc Godard, French movie director

1 GRAMMAR present perfect

a Write the sentences with contractions.

1 I have not read *The Pillars of the Earth*.
   I haven't read The Pillars of the Earth.

2 James has not seen this movie before.
   _____

3 They have gone to the movie theater tonight.
   _____

4 She has cried at a lot of movies.
   _____

5 I have bought all the Harry Potter movies.
   _____

6 They have not taken any photos.
   _____

7 He has interviewed a famous actor.
   _____

8 We have not appeared in a movie.
   _____

b Write sentences with the present perfect.

1 she / read / *The Help*
   She's read The Help   .

2 we / not see / this show
   We haven't seen this show   .

3 my parents / fall asleep
   _____ .

4 Adam / appear / in a movie
   _____ .

5 I / not speak to an actor
   _____ .

6 you / break / the camera
   _____ .

7 Dawn / not cry / at a movie
   _____ .

8 we / not forget / the tickets
   _____ .

c Complete the dialogue.

A ¹ _____*Have you heard*_____ (you / hear) of John le Carré?
B Yes, I ² _____ (read) some of his books.
A Really? Which books ³ _____ (you / read)
B I ⁴ _____ (read) *The Constant Gardener* recently. It was great!
A ⁵ _____ (you / see) the movie?

B No, but my brother ⁶ _____ (see) it. He loves John le Carré.
A ⁷ _____ (he / read) *Tinker, Tailor, Soldier, Spy*?
B Yes, and he ⁸ _____ (see) the movie.

2 VOCABULARY irregular past participles

a Write the simple past forms and past participles of these irregular verbs in the chart.

Infinitive	Simple past	Past participle
1 be	*was / were*	*been*
2 break		
3 do		
4 eat		
5 fall		
6 forget		
7 go		
8 leave		
9 sing		
10 speak		
11 take		
12 wear		

b Use past participles from the chart in **a** to complete the sentences.

1 Have you ever ___*sung*___ karaoke?
2 We've never _____ the movie theater before the end of a movie.
3 My sister has never _____ octopus before.
4 Has your brother ever _____ your birthday?
5 Have you ever _____ glasses?
6 I've never _____ my leg.
7 My friend hasn't _____ the homework.

3 PRONUNCIATION sentence stress

a **iChecker** Listen and <u>underline</u> the stressed words.

> A Have you read *The Millennium Trilogy*?
> B No, I haven't.
> A Have you seen the movies?
> B Yes, I have. I've seen all of them.

b **iChecker** Listen again and repeat the sentences. <u>Copy</u> the <u>rhy</u>thm.

4 READING

a Read the article about a movie adaptation of a book. Did fans prefer the ending in the book or the movie?

My Sister's Keeper

Fans of American author Jodi Picoult who have read her novel *My Sister's Keeper* get a big surprise when they see the movie. This is because the movie has a completely different ending from the book.

The novel tells the story of 13-year-old Anna Fitzgerald who was born to save the life of her older sister, Kate, who is very sick. Kate has cancer and Anna goes to hospital many times to give her sister blood and other things to keep Kate alive. However, when Anna is 13, she finds out that Kate needs one of her kidneys, and she decides that she doesn't want to give it to her. Anna goes to find a lawyer to help her fight her case in court.

At the end of the book, Anna wins her case so that in the future she can make her own decisions about her body. Unfortunately, the same day as she wins the case, she is in her lawyer's car when they have a serious accident. Anna is brain-dead after the crash, and the lawyer gives the doctors permission to use Anna's kidney. So in the end, Anna dies and Kate lives.

At the end of the movie, before they know the result of the court case, Kate and Anna's brother, Jesse, tells the family that Kate doesn't want to have any more operations. Kate dies and then Anna's lawyer visits the house to tell Anna she has won the case. So, in the movie Kate dies and Anna lives.

A website asked the people who have read the book and seen the movie to vote on the two different endings. 77% said that they hated the new ending while 13% said they preferred it to the ending in the book. Ten percent said that they enjoyed both the book and the movie and that the ending made no difference to them.

b Read the article again and choose a, b, or c.

1 Jodi Picoult is…
   a a lawyer.
   b a writer.
   c a doctor.
2 Anna's parents had Anna because…
   a they wanted another child.
   b they wanted to save their daughter.
   c they wanted another girl.
3 …dies at the end of the book.
   a The healthy sister
   b The sister who was sick
   c The brother
4 … dies at the end of the movie.
   a The healthy sister
   b The sister who was sick
   c The brother
5 … of the people who voted didn't think the ending was important.
   a 77%
   b 13%
   c 10%

5 LISTENING

a **iChecker** Listen to a radio program. Who wrote the two books? _____

b **iChecker** Listen again. Write T (true) or F (false).

1 *Great Expectations* was made in 1956.   *F*
2 The movie critic is going to talk about two movies.   __
3 *Great Expectations* is a black and white movie.   __
4 The main character in *Great Expectations* is a girl.   __
5 The movie is more frightening than the book.   __
6 The host has read the book *The English Patient*.   __
7 The author of *The English Patient* isn't American.   __
8 The main character in *The English Patient* had a car crash. __
9 The critic says that the best thing about the movie is the love story.   __
10 Both the book and the movie have won important prizes.   __

USEFUL WORDS AND PHRASES

Learn these words and phrases.

blood /blʌd/
appear /əˈpɪr/
at least /ət ˈlist/
fall asleep /fɔl əˈslip/
How about…? /ˈhaʊ əbaʊt/
order pizza /ˈɔrdər ˈpitsə/

I want to go somewhere I have never been, and I'd like to go there with you.

From The Hitchhiker's Guide to the Galaxy *by Douglas Adams, British writer*

12B I've never been there!

1 GRAMMAR present perfect or simple past?

a Complete the dialogues with the correct form of the verbs in parentheses.

1 **A** _Have you been_ (you / be) on vacation recently?
   B Yes, we have. We _____ (go) to the beach in July.

2 **A** When _____ (your brother / buy) his motorcyle?
   B Last week. My parents _____ (pay) for it.

3 **A** _____ (you / meet) your sister's new roommate?
   B Yes, I _____ (meet) her at a party last month.

4 **A** _____ (you / be) to New York?
   B Yes, I _____ (go) there last year.

5 **A** _____ (your parents / ever / give) you an expensive present?
   B Yes, I _____ (get) a car for my last birthday.

6 **A** Why _____ (he / send) his wife some flowers yesterday?
   B Because he _____ (forget) their anniversary.

b Complete the sentences with *gone* or *been*.

1 Has Clare _gone_ home? She isn't at her desk.
2 Have you ever _____ to Disneyland?
3 My sister isn't here because she's _____ for a walk.
4 My neighbors are away because they've _____ on vacation.
5 You look tan. Have you _____ to the beach?
6 It's late so the children have _____ to bed.
7 The refrigerator is full because we've _____ shopping.
8 Have you ever _____ to an Indian restaurant?
9 My best friend has never _____ abroad.
10 Jane's parents are out. They've _____ to the supermarket.

2 PRONUNCIATION irregular past participles

a Circle the word with a different vowel sound.

1 fish	2 saw	3 egg	4 up	5 train	6 phone
given	walk	left	come	taken	broken
written	call	heard	done	made	known
seen	ball	said	drunk	read	lost
driven	last	sent	got	paid	spoken

b **iChecker** Listen and check. Then listen and repeat the words.

3 VOCABULARY more irregular past participles

a Write the simple past forms and past participles of these irregular verbs in the chart.

Infinitive	Simple past	Past participle
1 buy	*bought*	*bought*
2 drink		
3 find		
4 give		
5 have		
6 hear		
7 know		
8 lose		
9 make		
10 meet		
11 pay		
12 send		
13 spend		
14 think		
15 win		

b Complete the sentences with past participles from the chart in **a**.

1 I'm going to be late. I've _lost_ the car keys.
2 Have you ever _____ long hair?
3 Debbie and Fernando have _____ a new house.
4 Kenji can't go out because he's _____ all his money.
5 My parents have never _____ of Maroon 5.
6 You've _____ a lot of mistakes.
7 She's _____ some money in the street.
8 He's _____ a lot of water today because it's so hot.

4 READING

a Read the email. Check (√) the places Jessica has been to.

_____ Arizona

_____ California

_____ Colorado

_____ New Mexico

_____ Oklahoma

_____ Texas

From: Jessica
To: Brianna
Subject: Hi from the US Southwest!

Dear Brianna,

Thanks for your email telling me all the news from home. I'm glad everyone is well and that you're not missing me too much!

We're more than half way through our trip around the US Southwest, and we're having a great time. We've stayed in four states so far, and now we're in Colorado. We spent three days in San Diego, California where we walked on the 3-mile long Mission Beach Boardwalk along the ocean. From San Diego, we drove to Las Vegas, Nevada where we spent two days seeing the sights. We even saw a show by Cirque du Soleil—an amazing live music, dancing, and circus show—in one of Las Vegas's many theaters. Our next stop was Phoenix, Arizona, which we found too hot—it was over 100 degrees Fahrenheit during the day. The best part of our visit was the Musical Instrument Museum, which has musical instruments from all over the world. From Phoenix we drove to Santa Fe, New Mexico, where we decided to relax and enjoy a spa. The weather was hot in Santa Fe, but not as hot as Phoenix! We wanted to stay longer, but it was time for us to drive to Colorado. And now here we are in Denver. Denver is a beautiful place with a lot of tall, modern buidlings. We've been to the Denver Zoo today, but unfortunately, it rained—just our luck.

We have one more day in Denver, and then we're going to drive to Tulsa. We haven't been to Oklahoma or Texas yet, so we're looking forward to the last part of our trip.

I'll write again when we get to Austin. Until then, take care and give my love to Mom and Dad.

Love,

Joanna

b Read the email again. Where did Jessica…?

1 see dancers _____

2 visit a museum _____

3 have a relaxing time _____

4 take a long walk _____

5 see animals _____

5 LISTENING

a **iChecker** Listen to four speakers talking about different places they have been to. Where did they go? When?

	Where?	When?
Speaker 1	_____	_____
Speaker 2	_____	_____
Speaker 3	_____	_____
Speaker 4	_____	_____

b **iChecker** Listen again. Who…?

1 did an extreme sport   Speaker ☐

2 was in a dangerous situation Speaker ☐

3 took part in a local celebration Speaker ☐

4 wasn't on vacation   Speaker ☐

USEFUL WORDS AND PHRASES

Learn these words and phrases.

recently /ˈrisntli/

romantic /roʊˈmæntɪk/

Let's forget it. /lɛts fərˈgɛt ɪt/

TV series /ti ˈvi sɪriz/

win (a cup or medal) /wɪn/

One Ring to rule them all, One Ring to find them,
One Ring to bring them all and in the darkness bind them.

From The Fellowship of the Ring *by J. R. R. Tolkien, British author*

12C The *American English File* questionnaire

1 GRAMMAR review

a Correct the mistakes in the second sentence.

1 Those are her children. They is very young.
   They are very young.

2 Jim lives in the city center. Your apartment is big.
   _____.

3 I went shopping yesterday. I bought a shirt new.
   _____.

4 That's Sophie. She's the sister of Ryan.
   _____.

5 We love the summer. We go on vacation on August.
   _____.

6 Tanya is going to lose her job. She always is late.
   _____.

7 I don't like karaoke. I can't to sing.
   _____.

8 My brother is late. I'm waiting for he.
   _____.

9 We're doing the housework. We don't mind clean.
   _____.

10 Our yard is small. There aren't some plants.
   _____.

11 The hotel was full. There was a lot of guests.
   _____.

12 They're very healthy. They don't eat many sugar.
   _____.

13 I'm 21. I'm more older than you.
   _____.

14 I don't like crocodiles. They're the more dangerous animals.
   _____.

15 Hannah likes languages. She speaks Chinese good.
   _____.

16 My sister has a good job. She's engineer.
   _____.

b Look at the **time expressions** and complete the sentences with the correct form of the verbs. Use the simple present, present continuous, simple past, present perfect, or *be going to*.

1 We **never** _have_ pizza for dinner. (have)
2 Caitlin _____ the dog for a walk **twice a day**. (take)
3 _____ you _____ your friends **last weekend**? (see)
4 They _____ **tomorrow** because Jack is sick. (not come)
5 _____ you **ever** _____ to South America? (be)
6 _____ your son _____ to drive **next year**? (learn)
7 We _____ meat **every day**. (not eat)
8 We _____ a movie **next Saturday**. (see)

9 _____ you **ever** _____ a famous person? (meet)
10 **Last night** my husband _____ dinner. (cook)
11 I think it _____ **tonight**. (rain)
12 What time _____ you **usually** _____ to bed on the weekend? (go)
13 My brother _____ soccer **right now**. (play)
14 We _____ to work **yesterday**. (not walk)
15 What _____ your daughter _____ **today**? (do)
16 I _____ **never** _____ that book, but I'd like to. (read)

2 VOCABULARY review: word groups

a Circle the word that is different.

1	Canada	Japanese	Turkey	China
2	Iran	Vietnam	Asia	Mexico
3	tall	expensive	dark	slim
4	lawyer	teacher	shower	waiter
5	aunt	daughter	niece	brother
6	spring	cloudy	snowy	windy
7	fireplace	cupboard	sofa	kitchen
8	mushroom	strawberries	onion	peas
9	pharmacy	department store	bridge	shopping mall

b Continue the series.

1 one, two, three, _four_
2 ten, twenty, _____
3 Monday, Tuesday, _____
4 first, second, _____
5 morning, afternoon, _____
6 once, twice, _____
7 summer, fall, _____
8 June, July, _____
9 second, minute, _____
10 day, week, _____

c Complete the phrases with verbs.

1 _listen_ to music
2 d_____ homework
3 s_____ hello
4 t_____ a shower
5 g_____ shopping
6 t_____ photos
7 h_____ a noise
8 g_____ dressed
9 h_____ two children
10 u_____ a computer

3 PRONUNCIATION review: sounds

a (Circle) the word with a different sound.

fish (i)	1	rich dirty big
tree (i)	2	bread peas meat
cat (æ)	3	safe black fat
car (ɑr)	4	dark day far
clock (ɑ)	5	money model doctor
saw (ɔ)	6	mall more met
bull (ʊ)	7	cook food good
boot (u)	8	who do go
bird (ər)	9	tired thirsty nurse
egg (ɛ)	10	**eat** healthy breakfast
train (eɪ)	11	paid steak said
bike (aɪ)	12	buy nice ring

b **iChecker** Listen and check.

c Underline the stressed syllable.

1 hos|pi|tal
2 ex|pen|sive
3 ma|ga|zine
4 head|phones
5 ad|mi|ni|stra|tor
6 en|gi|neer

7 I|tal|ian
8 Au|gust
9 di|ffi|cult
10 mu|si|cian
11 ga|rage
12 ba|na|nas

d **iChecker** Listen and check.

4 READING

Read the article and answer the questions.

THE MOVIES in *The Lord of the Rings* trilogy have had a big impact on New Zealand. The country has become "Middle Earth" to many of the people who have seen the movies. This comes as no surprise to the movie director Peter Jackson, who is in fact a New Zealander. He chose his home country because he knew that the variety of different landscapes made New Zealand the best place to shoot the movies.

Jackson and his team looked over the whole country for the most beautiful and most appropriate areas. The rolling hills of Matamata became Hobbiton, the village where Bilbo Baggins lives, and the volcanic region of Mount Ruapehu transformed into the fiery Mount Doom, where Sauron first made the Ring. In total, the team used 150 different locations all over New Zealand, and they spent 274 days filming.

Thirty of the locations Jackson used are national parks or conservation sites, so he needed to get special permission to film here. In some cases, a special team dug up the protected plants and took them to special nurseries, where they lived until filming finished. Then the team took them back to the park and replanted them again. In Queenstown, Jackson used enormous red rugs to protect the plants in the battle scenes because there were up to 1,100 people on set every day.

The *Lord of the Rings* movies have been so popular that the tourist industry in New Zealand has grown dramatically. Today, tour companies offer a wide range of tours to different locations of the movie, including Hobbiton, Mount Doom, and Edoras.

1 Who directed *The Lord of the Rings* movies?
2 Where is the director from?
3 Why did he choose New Zealand?
4 Which area did they use to create Mount Doom?
5 How many different locations did they use in total?
6 What was the problem with some of the locations?
7 How did they solve the problem?
8 Which locations from the movies can tourists visit today?

5 LISTENING

iChecker Listen to an advertisement for a day trip and complete the notes.

Lord of the Rings Edoras Tour			
Departure time:	Christchurch ¹ _9 a.m._	Lunch:	luxury ⁵_____
Return time:	Christchurch ²_____	Price:	
Transportation:	by ³_____	Adults:	⁶ $_____
Destination:	Mount ⁴_____ (Edoras)	Children:	⁷ $_____

Listening

7 A))

H = Host, **T** = Tom

H Hello, and welcome to what is a very special show, because we're going to find out the results of our poll. Tom Brewer from the Discovery Channel is here to tell us who the greatest American of all time is. Hello, Tom.

T Hi, there.

H So, let's look at the Top 5, Tom.

T All right. Well, number 5 on the list is, in fact, Ben Franklin.

H OK. I'm not surprised.

T I'm not either. Did you know that he was the owner of a newspaper, *The Pennsylvania Gazette*, at the age of 22? Or that he was an expert swimmer?

H No, I didn't know that! Very interesting! But who is number 4?

T Well, number 4 is George Washington.

H Ah, yes…George Washington. Tell us something about him.

T Well, he was born in Virginia on February 22, 1732. He was the first president of the US . He died in 1779 at the age of 67.

H OK. Who's next?

T Number 3 on the list is Martin Luther King, Jr.

H Yes, he was an amazing person.

T That's right. So let me tell you about him. He was born on January 15th, 1929 in Atlanta, Georgia. He was famous because he was one of the leaders of the US civil rights movement. He was killed on April 4th, 1968. He was only 39 years old.

H Yes, that was tragic. So, Number 2?

T Number 2 is Abraham Lincoln, the 12th president of the US.

H Really? Tell us about him.

T Well, he was born on February 12th in 1809. He was president during the American Civil War, and he was killed on April 15th, 1865. He wasn't very old when he died, only 56.

H OK…and now for the moment we've been waiting for. Who is the greatest American of all time? Who is at the top of the list?

T Well, I'll give you a clue. It's a man…he was born on February 6th, 1911 and died in 2004. He was an actor and a US president!

H I knew it! It's Ronald Reagan!

T That's right. Ronald Reagan is the greatest American of all time. Americans voted for Reagan because jobs were good and salaries were high when he was president.

H Tom Brewer, thank you so much for joining us.

T My pleasure.

7 B))

Speaker 1 I had a bad trip one vacation when I wanted to visit my family back home in Chicago. About twenty minutes after leaving the airport, there was a problem with our plane. We returned to the airport again and waited five hours for another plane. Finally, I arrived in Chicago eight hours later than I planned.

Speaker 2 We tried to go on vacation to Toronto one year, but it was a disaster. We started our trip late and stopped for lunch in a town on the way. When we were on the road after lunch, our car started making a strange noise and finally, it stopped altogether. The car ended up in a garage, and we called a taxi to take us home again.

Speaker 3 My bad trip happened when I was in college. I wanted to go home for the weekend, so I was on a train. The trip was very long – about seven hours – and I was almost home. We stopped at the last station before mine, but then we didn't start again. The train was broken. In the end, my dad picked me up in his car.

Speaker 4 I had a bad experience with a bus company once. I booked a ticket from the Port Authority Bus Terminal in New York City to Newark Airport, but there were a lot of people at the bus station when I arrived, and it was impossible to get on the bus. In the end, I traveled to the airport with a businessman in a taxi. He didn't ask me for any money, which was nice.

7 C))

I = Interviewer, **M** = Melissa

I Can you tell us about a memorable night, Melissa?

M Well, let me see. There are a lot of them, actually. But yes, there was one particular night this year that was memorable.

I When was it?

M It was February 14th.

I Valentine's Day?

M Yes. That's why I remember the date. It was Valentine's Day, but I didn't have a boyfriend at the time. In fact, I was with two friends.

I Where were you?

M I was in Miami. There was a concert that night by my favorite singer, Drake, so I traveled to Miami to see it.

I When did you arrive in Miami?

M The night before the concert.

I So, what did you do before the concert?

M We had a coffee at an interesting coffee shop near the beach. Then we tried to find the concert. We didn't know exactly where the theater was, so we drove around for a very long time. In the end, we got there five minutes before the concert started.

I Was the concert good?

M Yes, it was fantastic. Drake sang all our favorite songs, and we danced and sang for about two hours.

I Did you go home after the concert?

M No, we didn't go home right away. We didn't have dinner before it started, so we were hungry. We went to a fast-food restaurant and had a hamburger. It was delicious! After that, we drove home.

I What time did you get home?

M We didn't get home that late. It was two o'clock in the morning, more or less. But we had a great time. That was the important thing.

8 A))

H = Host, **D** = Detective

H Hello and welcome to *What Next?*, the program that looks at today's career opportunities. In the studio with us is Detective Jeremy Downs from the Metropolitan Police. He's here to tell us about his job and how he got it. Hello, Jeremy.

D Good morning, Peter.

H So, tell us, why did you decide to join the police?

D Well, it runs in my family, really. My dad was a detective, and so was his father. I always knew that this was what I wanted to do.

H What did you need to become a detective?

D First, I got a college degree in criminal justice. Then I had to get experience as a regular police officer. So I worked as a police officer for two years. Then I took two tests – one to test my knowledge of the law and one to test my physical fitness for the job.

H Detective, what do you like most about your job?

D Well, you feel great when you solve a mystery and find a murderer. That's the best thing about it. And also, I'm usually outside or talking to people, so I don't spend much time in an office. I'm never bored when I'm working.

H And what don't you like about it?

D It's a very stressful job. I'm usually working on more than one case at a time, and sometimes it's difficult to know what to do first. And going to the scene of a murder can be terrible. But apart from that, I love my job and I recommend it to anyone who likes finding answers and solving problems.

H Detective Downs, thank you for joining us.

8 B))

M = Mrs. Goodings, **J** = Joanna, **B** = Bradley

M Hello. Good morning. I'm Mrs. Goodings.

J Hi. I'm Joanna, and this is Bradley.

B Hi.

M Hello. Please come in. So…let's start, OK? This is the kitchen, as you can see.

B It's very big.

M Yes. There isn't a dining room, so we eat in here.

J Oh look! The walls are big windows! You can see the yard – it's beautiful!

B Can I ask you a question, Mrs. Goodings? Why did we come in the back door?

M We always use the back door. There isn't a rug in the kitchen so there aren't any problems with dirty shoes.

B Oh. Right.

J Where's the washing machine?

M It's in the corner over there.

J Oh, yes. I see it. Why is there a hole in the ceiling?

M Well, upstairs is the bathroom. The hole is for when you take a shower. You take off your clothes and put them down the hole. They land on the floor next to the washing machine.

J Oh. That's interesting!

M Yes…It was my idea…Now…this way please…I want to show you the living room. There. What do you think?

J Oh! There are big windows here, too. I love it!

B Mrs. Goodings, is there a television?

M No, there isn't. My husband and I don't watch TV. We prefer listening to music. Now…let's go upstairs.

J There are four bedrooms upstairs, is that right?

M Yes. Four bedrooms and a bathroom.

B Is this the bathroom?

M Yes, it is. Be careful with the…

B Aargh!!!

J Bradley? Bradley? Where is he?

M Don't worry. He's in the kitchen.

J What?

M Do you remember the hole in the ceiling?

J Oh, no! Bradley? Bradley? Are you all right?

8 C))

Speaker 1 When I was in Costa Rica, I stayed in a bed-and-breakfast hotel with a difference. It was in the middle of the jungle and we could see monkeys and birds from our window. As well as an air-conditioned bedroom, there was a full bathroom with a warm-water shower. We had a small refrigerator and a coffeemaker, too.

Speaker 2 I spent the night in an ice hotel when I was in the north of Sweden. The temperature in the room was 23°F and the only furniture was a bed made of ice and snow. I slept in a special sleeping bag with all my clothes on – I even wore a hat! It wasn't very comfortable, really, because there wasn't even a bathroom!

Speaker 3 I once stayed in a very artsy hotel when I was in Berlin. All of the rooms in the hotel were completely different. In the middle of my room there was a diamond-shaped bed and when I lay down, I could see hundreds of people who looked just like me. There weren't any cupboards, so I put my bags under the bed.

Speaker 4 I went to Fiji with my husband after we got married and we stayed in a really special hotel. A special elevator took us down to our room, which was surrounded by fish and other sea animals. There was a large, comfortable bed in the bedroom and a library and personal office in the living room. We loved it there!

9 A))

Speaker 1 My favorite meal is roast beef. It sounds boring really – just a piece of meat, but you need to cook it for the right amount of time. My mom cooks it perfectly and she always serves it with roasted potatoes and a lot of other vegetables – peas, carrots, broccoli, and beans. Then she pours a sauce called gravy all over it. Delicious!

Speaker 2 Indian food is really popular these days, and I absolutely love it! We're lucky because we have a great Indian restaurant down the street. My favorite dish is chicken tikka masala, which is chicken in a sauce made with tomatoes, cream, and spices. I always order special Indian bread to eat it with.

Speaker 3 You probably think I'm crazy, but one of my favorite meals is a hot dog and French fries. Yes, I know it's not very healthy, but I only have it about twice a month. I always buy it from the same street vendor, and if the weather's nice, I sit outside in the park to eat it. I put a lot of mustard and relish on the hot dog. Yum!!!

Speaker 4 My favorite food is Chinese food, and I always order the same dish – sweet and sour tofu and vegetables. This is pieces of tofu in a sauce made of sugar, tomatoes, white vinegar, and soy sauce. The sauce also has pineapple, green peppers, and onion in it. I always eat it with rice. I have it at the restaurant, and sometimes I get it to go and eat it at home.

9 B))

H = Host, **M** = Miriam

H Hello and welcome to the program. Our first guest today is nutritionist Miriam Shepherd. She's here to give us some advice about healthy eating. Miriam, what do we need to eat to be healthy?

M Well, basically, we all need a balanced diet.

H And what exactly is a balanced diet?

M It's when you eat the right amount of food from each of the five different food groups.

H Can you tell us more about those groups, Miriam?

M Yes, of course. Let's start with carbohydrates. These are things like bread, pasta, rice, and potatoes. We need to eat a lot of carbohydrates because they give us energy.

H OK. What's next?

M The next group is fruit and vegetables. Things like apples and oranges, and peas and carrots. These contain important vitamins, so you need to eat something from this group at every meal.

H OK. What's the third group?

M The third group is protein, which is in food like meat and eggs. We need it to grow and to repair the body. You need to eat a lot of foods from this group, but not necessarily with every meal.

H Interesting. What's the next group, Miriam?

M Milk and dairy. Dairy foods are things like cheese and yogurt. This group contains calcium, which is important for our bones and teeth. But you have to be a little careful because they sometimes contain a lot of fat. You need to eat something from this group every day, but not necessarily every meal.

H And which is the last group, Miriam?

M The last group is fats and sugars. These are found in snacks, like cake, cookies, candy, and chips. Fats and sugars aren't very good for you, so only eat a little food from this group – maybe once or twice a week.

H Thank you, Miriam. That was very helpful.

M My pleasure.

9 C))

M = Michael, **R** = Rachel

M Rachel, did you know that there are two cities called Birmingham?

R Really? I know the one in the state of Alabama in the US, but where's the other one?

M It's in the UK.

R OK. Are the cities very small?

M Not really. One big difference is the population. There are only 243,000 people living in Birmingham in the US, whereas there are over a million in Birmingham in the UK.

R So, Birmingham in the UK is bigger then?

M Well, no. The area of Birmingham in the UK is 63 square miles while Birmingham in the US covers 93.8 square miles.

R Oh, that's big.

M Yes, but there aren't as many people. Birmingham in the UK isn't very green.

R And the American Birmingham is really green.

M Yes. And there's also a big difference in age. Birmingham in the UK was already a small village as early as the seventh century while Birmingham in the US didn't exist until 1871.

R OK. What about the weather? It's always raining over here so the weather is probably better in Birmingham in the UK.

M You're right! There are 26 inches of rain in Birmingham in the UK. There is twice as much in Birmingham in the US—53 inches.

R Interesting!

M Yes, but it's colder over there. The average temperature in Birmingham in the US is 73° F whereas in Birmingham in the UK it's 55° F. That's ten degrees colder.

R So, why are you telling me all this anyway?

M I'm reading an article in the newspaper. It's about a mistake that they made in Birmingham. That's Birmingham in the UK, not ours.

R What happened?

M They made an advertisement for Birmingham in the US, but they used the wrong photo. They put a photo of Birmingham in the US on the advertisement instead of Birmingham in the UK.

R No! How funny!

M Yes, I thought so, too!

10 A))

H = Host, **M** = Max

H Hello, and welcome to the travel section of the program. Our guest today is travel writer Max Miller, whose book *Superlative Sights* came out yesterday. Max, welcome to the program.

M Thank you, Gloria.

H So what exactly is your book about?

M Well, it's basically about the biggest, the best, and the most beautiful places in the world.

H Can you give us some examples?

M Yes, of course. Let's start with Ayers Rock in Australia. Its other name is Uluru, and it's the world's largest rock. It's almost 12,000 feet long, 7,920 feet wide, and 1,141 feet high – enormous!

H Yes, I see what you mean. What else?

M How about the world's highest waterfall? Angel Falls in Venezuela is 3,212 feet high. A lot of the water evaporates before it hits the ground.

H Wow! Are there only natural places in your book, or do you have any man-made structures?

M Yes, we include man-made structures, too. For example, do you know what the tallest building is right now?

H No…tell us more.

M Well, it's Burj Khalifa in Dubai in the United Arab Emirates. It stands 2,717 feet high.

H Incredible!

M What about the oldest city in the world?

H I'm not sure. Um…somewhere in Egypt?

M Almost, but not quite. It's Aleppo, in Syria. The city dates back to 600 B.C. and it's the oldest continuously inhabited city in the world.

H Really? I didn't know that.

M There are also some interesting facts about transportation. For instance, do you know anything about the longest train trip?

H Well, I suppose it's in Russia.

M That's right. The Trans-Siberian Railway from Moscow to Vladivostok is 5,771 miles long and crosses seven different time zones.

H That's one long train ride!

M That's right. And how about plane trips? What's the shortest runway in the world?

H Runway? You mean where the planes land at the airport?

M That's right.

H I have no idea.

M Well, it's on the beautiful island of Saba in the Caribbean. The runway is only 1,300 feet long and it ends in a 196-foot drop into the ocean.

H This is fascinating stuff, Max. I can't wait to read your book!

10 B)))

Speaker 1 I had my first experience CouchSurfing in China. I wanted to spend a few days in a city called Guilin, so I made contact with a Chinese guy named Leo. Leo was the perfect host: he gave me a bed, he organized a dinner that other CouchSurfers came to, and he showed me around the city. I loved it, and I'd recommend it to anyone!

Speaker 2 My first CouchSurfing experience did not go well. I was in Boston – in the state of Massachusetts in the US, and I found a college student who agreed to host me. First, he was late and then he didn't stop talking about himself all night. In the end, I said I was tired and went to bed. The next morning, I left Boston and took the train to New York City, where my host was an older woman, and I had a much better time.

Speaker 3 I'm Canadian, and my first CouchSurfing experience was in New Orleans in the state of Louisiana in the US. I wanted to do some research for a novel I'm writing, so I needed to meet as many people as possible. My sister told me about the website, so I decided to try it out. In the end, I stayed with someone different every night, and I got a lot of ideas for my book!

Speaker 4 I was in Australia working when I found out about the CouchSurfing website. I wanted to travel around the country on weekends, but I didn't know anyone. A friend suggested looking at the CouchSurfing website, and I'm very happy that I did. I now have friends all over Australia, and some of them are going to visit me in the US when I go back next month.

10 C)))

P = Pete, A = Amy

P Amy, do you remember Uri Geller?
A No, I don't. Who is he?
P He is a kind of psychic. He was on TV a lot in the past and he became famous.
A What kind of tricks did he do?
P Well, his most famous trick was bending spoons. There's a photo here – come and take a look.
A Oh, there's a video here, too, on YouTube. Let's watch it.
P You see? At first, the spoon looks normal. Here, he's touching it with his finger…and now, it's bent.
A That's amazing!
P Actually…it isn't.
A What?
P It's a trick.
A So how does he do it?
P The spoon is bent before he shows it to us. He's hiding the bent part in his hand, so that you think it's a normal spoon. You don't have much time to look at the spoon at all because he's talking so much. What he's doing is distracting you while he's pulling the bent spoon slowly out of his hand. You think he's bending it but, in fact, he isn't.
A So, the guy is a cheater!
P Yes, but he's a very famous cheater.
A Does he still do his trick in public?
P Yes, he does. And the most incredible thing is that people still believe it.

11 A)))

Speaker 1: Toronto, Canada

On the weekend, the city is pretty busy. It's very similar to New York City or Washington, D.C. The streets are crowded with cars and people. There are interesting neighborhoods to visit, great restaurants to eat at, and a lot of places to hear music. I think most people stay in the city because there isn't much to do outside of the city.

People dress nicely here, especially at work. In big companies, it's normal for men to wear suits and women to wear business clothes. On the weekend, people dress more casually. They wear jeans or shorts and T-shirts, depending on the weather.

An interesting thing is that Toronto's nickname is "Hollywood North." A lot of TV and movie companies film their shows in Toronto. The city is also home to the Toronto International Film Festival. Only the Cannes Film Festival in France is bigger!

Speaker 2: Reykjavik, Iceland

In Iceland, a very important part of life is swimming and going to a hot tub, which is like a small swimming pool with hot water. People go before work or on the weekend to meet with their friends, or sometimes even to have business meetings!

The countryside in Iceland is incredible. There are almost no trees, and there are volcanoes and fields of lava, which are the incredibly hot stones that come out of the volcanoes. You can walk for days and not see another person, because there aren't many people in Iceland. In Reykjavik, there are less than 250,000 people, and the second-biggest city has only 15,000.

Icelandic people are very creative. It's normal for many people to make music, paint or draw, and even write books. Also, many people make their own clothes, and they look really fashionable!

11 B)))

H = Host, D = Dave, C = Carolina, E = Eddie

H Hello. I'm Jenny Richards, and I'm on the streets of New York City asking people what they want to do with their lives. Let's start with this man over here. Hello.
D Hi.
H I'm Jenny Richards from TV NYC. What's your name?
D I'm Dave.
H OK, Dave, we'd like to ask you about your ambitions for the future. What do you want to do with your life?
D Well, uh, what I'd really like, um, is…
H Yes?
D I'd really like to buy a motorcycle. I had a little dirt bike when I was younger, but I stopped riding it when I got married and had kids. Now, I'd like to start again.
H Well, good luck with your ambition, Dave. Let's talk to someone else now. Hello. What's your name?
C Carolina.
H So, what do you want to do with your life, Carolina?
C Well, I'd love to go traveling to different places.
H Oh really? Any particular place?
C Yes. I'd really like to go to Australia with my sister. I have friends there, and it's a very exciting country.
H Why don't you, then?

C I can't.
H Why not?
C My sister hates flying, and it's a 22-hour flight.
H Well, maybe one day you can go there on your own. Good luck with your ambition, Carolina. Now, what about you? What's your name?
E I'm Eddie.
H Do you have any ambitions, Eddie?
E I'd like to see Kings of Leon live.
H Why Kings of Leon?
E They're my favorite band.
H Why don't you get a ticket for their next concert?
E Yeah, I want to, but they aren't touring this year. They're making a new album.
H Well, maybe next year. Now, let's talk to this woman over here…

11 C)))

Speaker 1 I really couldn't live without the Internet. Every evening after dinner, I spend a few hours on my laptop playing games online. My job is very stressful, so it helps me relax. I forget about my problems and focus on something different. I think it's really good for me.

Speaker 2 The Internet is really important for me because I live abroad. All of my family and friends live in the US, and I'm living in the UK. Phone calls are really expensive, but with the Internet I can Skype them whenever I want to. With Skype I can even see their faces, so it's much better than a phone call.

Speaker 3 Well, um, I'm a webmaster, so the Internet is very important for my job. I work with different websites, first of all creating them and then making sure that everyone can use them. I also try to make existing websites work faster. I enjoy my job because I love computers and solving problems.

Speaker 4 Yeah, I spend a lot of time on the Internet every day. It's a great way to keep in touch with friends and also to meet new people. There's one site I use a lot to talk to my friends, upload photos, and post videos that I find funny. I also like looking at my friends' profiles to see what they're doing.

12 A)))

H = Host, C = Christopher

H Hello, and welcome to *Movie Madness*. In the studio with us today is movie critic Christopher Phillips. We've asked him to choose his two favorite movie adaptations of books. Christopher, where are you going to start?
C Well, it's been a difficult choice but I'm going to start with a very early movie, the 1946 adaptation of *Great Expectations* by Charles Dickens.
H 1946? That is early.
C Yes, and as you can imagine, the movie is in black and white. It tells the story of a poor young boy named Pip who with the help of a mysterious person, becomes a gentleman. The story doesn't change much in the movie, but the photography makes the atmosphere darker and more frightening. It's an excellent adaptation.
H *Great Expectations*. OK. I haven't seen the movie, but I've read the book, of course. What's your other movie, Christopher?
C Well, my other choice is more recent. It's *The English Patient*.

H Yes, I've seen that one a few times. But I don't know anything about the book. Tell us more.

C Well, the author is a Sri Lankan-Canadian writer named Michael Ondaatje, and his novel won an important prize – the Booker Prize. The movie came out in 1996, and it's a wonderful adaptation of the book. It tells the story of a man in a military hospital who has been in a plane crash. We also learn something about the life and loves of his nurse. Again, there are a few changes to the story, but the best thing about the movie is the choice of actors, who are perfect for their parts. The movie won a total of nine Oscars, which shows just how good it is.

H Christopher Phillips, thank you for joining us.

C Thank you for having me. I've enjoyed it.

12 D))

Speaker 1 I = Interviewer, **S** = Speaker 1

I Have you ever been to Africa?

S Yes, I have. I've been to Kenya.

I When did you go?

S I went in 2010. We stayed with some friends who are living in Nairobi. While we were there, we went on a trip to Tsavo East, which is an enormous national park. Unfortunately, our car broke down in the park, and the guards took six hours to rescue us. It was really scary!

Speaker 2 I = Interviewer, **S** = Speaker 2

I Have you ever been to South America?

S Yes, I have. I've been to Brazil.

I When did you go?

S I went there in 2006 on a business trip. In fact, we were at a conference, so it wasn't very hard work. We stayed in a five-star hotel, and the company paid for everything.

Speaker 3 I = Interviewer, **S** = Speaker 3

I Have you ever been to Australia?

S Well, I haven't been to Australia, but I've been to New Zealand.

I When did you go?

S I went with my wife when we got married in 2011. We stayed in a luxury apartment on the banks of Lake Wakatipu, and we had a great time doing a lot of different water sports. The best moment for me, though, was when we did a bungee jump from the Kawarau Bridge. It was really exciting!

Speaker 4 I = Interviewer, **S** = Speaker 4

I Have you ever been to Asia?

S Yes, I have. I've been to Thailand.

I When did you go?

S I went with my family in 2006. We stayed in a special hotel in the jungle, and we slept in a treehouse. But the most amazing part of our trip happened when we visited Bangkok. We were lucky enough to be there for Songkran, the Thai New Year, so we saw the water festival. You know, the one where everybody throws water at each other in the street!

12 C))

New Zealand. Home of Middle Earth. And the best way to experience it is on our *Lord of the Rings* Edoras tour. The tour leaves Christchurch at 9 a.m. and returns at 6 p.m., but we can pick you up at other central city locations, too. The groups are small, and the guides are friendly and informative. You don't need to be a *Lord of the Rings* fan to enjoy the tour because the scenery is fantastic. Transportation is in a Land Rover, and we take you through the spectacular mountains of the Southern Alps where you can see clear lakes and blue rivers, and you can breathe fresh mountain air. Our destination is Mount Sunday, the real-life mountain that in the movie is Edoras, the capital city of the Rohan people. While you're there, you can use some the most famous items from the movie; Aragorn's sword, Gimli's axe, and the flag of Rohan. For lunch, there is a luxury picnic, which we eat outside in the open air. Visit our store at the end of your trip and buy exclusive Lord of the Rings souvenirs for your family and friends back home.

The tour runs daily throughout the year, and you can buy tickets online. The price includes your pick up and drop off, your trip in the Land Rover, your guided walk to the very top of Edoras, and your delicious lunch. Tickets cost $135 for adults, per person, and $94 for children aged 14 and under.

So, what are you waiting for? Book your tickets now before you miss your chance to see one of the most beautiful *Lord of the Rings* locations. It's an experience you'll never forget.

OXFORD
UNIVERSITY PRESS

198 Madison Avenue
New York, NY 10016 USA

Great Clarendon Street, Oxford, OX2 6DP,
United Kingdom

Oxford University Press is a department of the University of Oxford. It furthers the University's objective of excellence in research, scholarship, and education by publishing worldwide. Oxford is a registered trade mark of Oxford University Press in the UK and in certain other countries

© Oxford University Press 2013

General Manager: Laura Pearson
Executive Publishing Manager: Erik Gundersen
Senior Managing Editor: Louisa van Houten
Associate Editor: Yasuko Morisaki
Associate Editor: Hana Yoo
Design Director: Susan Sanguily
Executive Design Manager: Maj-Britt Hagsted
Associate Design Manager: Michael Steinhofer
Senior Designer: Yin Ling Wong
Electronic Production Manager: Julie Armstrong
Production Artists: Elissa Santos,
Julie Sussman-Perez
Image Manager: Trisha Masterson
Image Editors: Liaht Pashayan, Joe Kassner
Production Coordinator: Brad Tucker

ISBN: 978 0 19 477623 3
MULTI-PACK B (PACK)

ISBN: 978 0 19 475587 8
STUDENT BOOK/WORKBOOK B (PACK COMPONENT)

ISBN: 978 0 19 476670 7
ICHECKER CD-ROM (PACK COMPONENT)

Printed in China

This book is printed on paper from certified and well-managed sources

STUDENT BOOK ACKNOWLEDGEMENTS

Cover Design: Yin Ling Wong

The authors and publisher are grateful to those who have given permission to reproduce the following extracts and adaptations of copyright material:

Illustrations by: Cover: Chellie Carroll; Peter Bull Studios: p.10, 58, 90, 103, 149; Annelie Carlstrom/AgencyRush: p.100; Echo Chernik/Illustration Ltd: p.80 - 81; Jonathan Burton: p.65, 66, 161, 162; Mark Duffin: p.17, 68; Dermot Flynn: p.8, 47, 95, 102, 107; Alex Green/Folio Art: p.62; Atushi Hara/Dutch Uncle agency: pp.4, 5, 55, 126, 127, 133, 134, 135, 142, 143, 156, 160; Satoshi Hashimoto/Dutch Uncle Agency: p. 131, 140, 141, 147, 150; Sophie Joyce: p.7, 12, 13, 70; Tim Marrs: pp.6, 72, 87; Jerome Mireault/Colagene: p.16 - 17; Gaku Nakagawa/Dutch Uncle Agency: p.38; Gavin Reece: p.45; James Taylor/Debut Art: pp.22. Pronunciation chart artwork: by Ellis Nadler

We would also like to thank the following for permission to reproduce the following photographs: Cover: Gemenacom/shutterstock.com; Andrey_Popov/shutterstock.com; Wavebreakmedia/shutterstock.com; Image Source/Getty Images; Lane Oatey/Blue Jean Images/Getty Images; BJI/Blue Jean Images/Getty Images; Image Source/Corbis; Yuri Arcurs/Tetra Images/Corbis; Wavebreak Media Ltd./Corbis; p6 Graphi-Ogre/Oxford University Press; p7 Frederic Lucano/Getty Images (woman); p7 Nick Dolding/Getty Images (couple); p7 Blend Images/Alamy (man); p9 Leigh Schindler/Getty Images (man); p9 Lucas Lenci/Corbis UK Ltd. (woman); p12 RDNL.Courtesy of The Roald Dahl Museum/The Roald Dahl Museum and Story Centre (Roald Dahl); p12 MM Studios (books); p12 Eamonn McCabe/Eamonn

McCabe - photographer (armchair); p14 Graphi-Ogre/Oxford University Press (iran); p14 Cameron Davidson/Corbis UK Ltd. (liberty); p14 Richard Michael Pruitt/Dallas/Alamy (airplane); p14 Jean-Pierre Lescourret/Corbis UK Ltd. (Empire State); p14 Corbis/Oxford University Press (sky); p14 D.Hurst/Alamy (baloon); p14 James and James/Photodsic/Getty Images (cheeseburger); p14 Photodisc/Oxford University Press (WhiteHouse); p14 Design Pics Inc/Photolibrary Group (lockers); p14 ignazuri/Alamy (jeans); p14 Buena Vista Images/Getty Images (taxi); p15 WireImage/Getty Images (Depp); p15 Alberto E.Rodriguez/Getty Images (Cruz); p17 Dimitrios Kaisaris/Shutterstock; p19 Image Farm/Oxford University Press (American); p19 EyeWire/Oxford University Press (British); p20 Richard Broadwell/Alamy; p21 EtiAmmos/Shutterstock (background); p21 Tim Boyle/Getty Images (car); p21 Gary Saxe/Shutterstock (tree); p21 Jon Hicks/Corbis UK Ltd. (traffic); p21 Alamy (burger); p21 VisionsofAmerica/Joe Sohm/Getty Images (rollercoaster); p22 Clarence Holmes Photography/Alamy (police car); p22 Geraint Lewis/Alamy (taxi); p23 Cultura/Photolibrary Group (pharmacist); p23 Ron Levine/Getty Images (girl); p25 Mika/Corbis UK Ltd.; p28 Larry Busacca/Getty Images (Bieber); p28 AFP/Getty Images (wristband); p28 Hubert Boesl/dpa/Corbis UK Ltd. (bowtie); p28 Corbis UK Ltd. (unicef); p28 Sipa Press/Rex Features (sunglasses); p28 Larry Busacca/Getty Images (tie); p29 Sipa Press/Rex Features (Bruni); p29 AFP/Getty Images (Clooney); p29 Hubert Boesl/dpa/Corbis UK Ltd. (Nicholson); p29 Corbis UK Ltd. (Messi); p29 moodboard/Alamy (man purple shirt); p29 Bloomberg via Getty Images/Getty Images (iphone a); p29 Corbis Bridge/Alamy (family); p29 Bloomberg via Getty Images/Getty Images (iphone b); p30 Oxford University Press (man); p30 Glow Images/Photolibrary Group (girl); p31 Image Source/Photolibrary Group (basketball); p31 Oxford University Press (chef); p32 Peter Cade/Getty Images; p33 Chris Willson/Alamy (boat); p33 John Warburton-Lee Photography/Alamy (lake); p33 CuboImages srl/Alamy (woman); p35 luchschen/Shutterstock (pizza); p35 Drive Images/Alamy (truck); p37 Brian Ach/WireImage for Clear Channel/Getty Images (Kelly); p37 Startraks Photo/Rex Features (Lee); p37 pdesign/Shutterstock (silhouette); p37 Startraks Photo/Rex Features (Carrie); p37 Arnold Turner/WireImage for BET Network/Getty Images (Ruben); p39 Patrick Syww/Alamy; p40 Alan Schmidt/iStockphoto; p41 P.Spiro/Alamy (ice skating); p41 iStockphoto/Thinkstock (columns); p41 Richard Green/Alamy (walkway); p41 Hemis/Corbis UK Ltd. (skyline); p42 D.Hurst/Alamy (jeans); p42 Jonathan Kantor/Lifesize/Getty Images (denim shirt); p42 Thomas Northcut/Photodisc/Getty Images (shoes); p42 Leonid Nyshko/Alamy (jacket); p42 Jonathan Kantor/Lifesize/Getty Images (grey trousers); p42 Tom Schierlitz/Getty Images (t-shirt); p42 Howard Shooter/Getty Images (skirt); p43 D.Hurst/Alamy (jeans); p43 Tom Schierlitz/Getty Images (t-shirt); p43 Tom Schierlitz/Getty Images (jacket); p46 Barry Lewis/In Pictures/Corbis UK Ltd.; p47 Tig Photo/Alamy (asparagus); p47 National Geographic Image Collection/Alamy (fireworks); p47 Design Pics Inc/Photolibrary Group (autumn); p48 Jonathan Kitchen/Photodisc/Getty Images (guitar); p48 Fernando Aceves/epa/Corbis UK Ltd. (Domingo); p48 Stockbyte/Getty Images (drum); p48 Popperfoto/Getty Images (Armstrong); p48 James Palmer/Retna Ltd./Corbis UK Ltd. (beyonce); p48 Dorling Kindersley/Getty Images (violin); p49 Sigi Tischler/epa/Corbis UK Ltd. (conductor); p49 Jennifer Taylor/Corbis UK Ltd. (orchestra); p51 Michael Blann/Getty Images; p52 Nat. Portrait Gall. Smithsonian/Art Resource/Photo Scala, Florence; p53 Bruce Davidson/Magnum Photos (Supremes); p53 Nat. Portrait Gall. Smithsonian/Art Resource/Photo Scala, Florence (Edison); p53 Nat. Portrait Gall. Smithsonian/Art Resource/Photo Scala, Florence (Marilyn); p54 Trinity Mirror/Alamy (house); p54 Dave Thompson/Getty Images (women); p54 Neil Tingle/Alamy (stadium); p56 Stockbyte/Getty Images (sunset); p56 Greg Allen/Rex Features (actors); p56 Justin Lane/epa/Corbis UK Ltd. (fans); p56 David Osuna/Demotix/Corbis UK Ltd (fans); p57 Radius Images/Photolibrary Group; p60 Westend61 GmbH/Alamy (woman); p60 Jason Hetherington/Getty Images (man); p60 Brownstock/Alamy (red book); p60/61 Philippa Lewis/Edifice/Arcaid/Corbis UK Ltd. (house); p60/61 Eric van den Brulle/Getty Images (open book); p61 Robert Recker/Corbis UK Ltd. (old woman); p61 Image Source/Photolibrary Group (young woman); p61 Awilli/Corbis UK Ltd. (man); p62 Philippa Lewis/Edifice/Arcaid/Corbis UK Ltd.; p64 John Robertson/Alamy (background); p64 John Robertson/Alamy (solid); p65 Comlongon Castle (female ghost); p65 Gosforth Hall Hotel (male ghost); p65 Gosforth Hall Hotel (bed); p67 Hulton-Deutsch Collection/Corbis UK Ltd.; p68 Todd Williamson/WireImage/Getty Images (Jennifer); p68 Noel Vasquez/Getty Images for Extra/Getty Images (Selita); p68 Martin Roe ./Retna Ltd./Corbi/Corbis UK Ltd. (Nacho); p69 Brownstock/Alamy (strawberry); p69 Michael Blann/Digital Vision/Getty Images (tomato); p69 Glow Asia/Photolibrary Group (chopsticks); p69 mediablitzimages (uk) Limited/Alamy (cookies); p69 Masterfile UK Ltd. (onion); p71 Stockbyte/Getty Images (scales); p71 Photocuisine/Masterfile UK Ltd. (sugar); p73 Ben Hider/Getty Images (Ken); p73 Sony Pictures Film Clips (Jeopardy); p73 c.20thC.Fox/Everett/Rex Features (Smarter); p73 c.ABC Inc/Everett/Rex Features (Millionaire); p76 Iain Masterton/Alamy (Mona Lisa); p76 Paulo Ferreira/Getty Images (bridge); p76 Sergio Ballivian/Getty Images (mountain); p76 Victor Fraile/Corbis UK Ltd. (Tiananmen); p76 Chad Ehlers/Getty Images (Buenos Aires); p76 Robert Holmes/Corbis UK Ltd. (station); p77 Travelscape Images/Alamy; p78 NetPhotos/Alamy (coach); p78 GlowImages/Alamy (map); p78 ImageState/Alamy (coach); p79 Iria Gonzalez-Liaño (woman); p79 SNEHIT/Shutterstock (desert); p79 Zooid Pictures (safa); p83 Eye Ubiquitous/Rex Features; p84 Visions LLC/Photolibrary Group (Atlanta); p84 Birger Lallo/Nordic Photos/Photolibrary Group (malmo); p84 Lonely Planet Images/Alamy (Valencia);